All of us need it.

Many need it for purpose.
Some need it for perception.

It is often displayed in public.

It is rarely used in private.

Some use it for power.
Many use it for profit.

All of us use it.

Beat Kaspar Baudenbacher was born and raised in Switzerland. He graduated from Art Center College of Design in Pasadena, CA, with a BFA in Graphic Design. As Co-Founder and Chief Creative Officer of Loyalkaspar, he has led its journey from a boutique animation studio to one of the leading branding agencies in the American entertainment media space with clients like—DISNEY, NETFLIX, CNN, HBO, ABC, DISCOVERY, MTV, PARAMOUNT+, NBC, ESPN, HULU, USA, SYFY, PEACOCK, STARZ, COMEDY CENTRAL, and MARVEL, among others.

He spends his days obsessing over what it takes for brands to tell cohesive and compelling stories across an ever-expanding universe of content.

And he spends his nights contemplating the effects of those brands on their audiences and how the two interact with each other.

He lives in Brooklyn, NY, with his wife and two sons.

AUTHOR PHOTOGRAPH BY
TOBIAS PRASSE

**FAST
COMPANY**
Press

somewhere yes

THE SEARCH FOR BELONGING IN A WORLD SHAPED BY BRANDING

WRITTEN & DESIGNED BY
BEAT KASPAR BAUDENBACHER

For my family.
Where I belong.

WHO AM I? WHO AM I? WHO AM I? WHO AM I? WHO AM I? WHO AM I?

+

My name is Beat ("Bay-Yacht").

I was born and raised in Switzerland, into a language that remains, to this day, strangely foreign to me. I struggled to inhabit a name—a label—that's not very common but distinctively Swiss.

I don't know that either of those circumstances led me to find refuge in visual communication, but it seems plausible.

I am fairly certain that they—in addition to my mother introducing me to life and work as an artist—made me fall in love with branding: *the peculiar art and science of distilling something down to its essence and giving it physical shape.*

Brands continue to shape humanity in ever more fundamental ways—even those of us who don't torment themselves over logos, typography, and message the way I do.

Brands connect us, just as they drive us apart.

At a time when it seems increasingly difficult to rely on our elected leaders, when virus and violence remind us of our shared mortality and required humility, we need to focus on brands that bring us together.

Brands touch almost every aspect of our lives, which is why this journey has taken me outside my comfort zone into topics far beyond my job description.

I am an expert in branding, not science, religion, or anthropology. But I view each and every one of these topics through the lens of symbols and message. And that's how all of this material connects for me.

My hope is to start conversations and inspire critical thinking while hopefully telling an engaging story.

Thank you for going on this adventure with me.

What does it mean to belong?

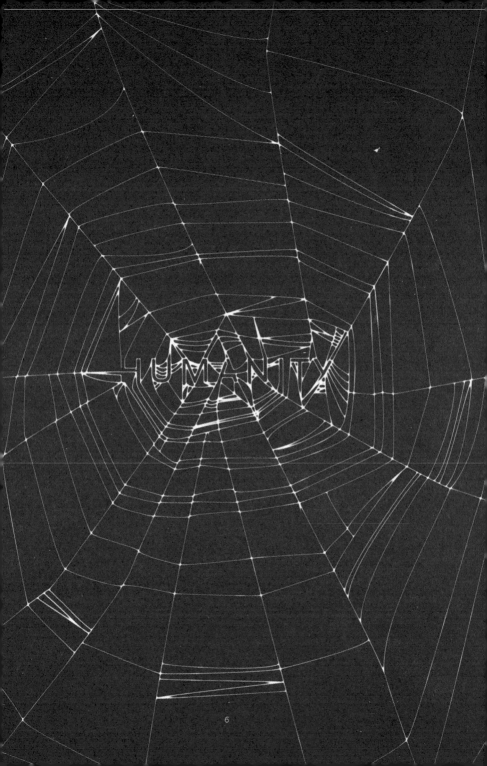

Humanity is a web.

It is a complex, intricately woven structure of cultures, races, and genders. A patchwork of beliefs, histories, worldviews, and identities. A quilt of sublime beauty and unimaginable horror.

We are all part of one species, sharing one planet.

And we inhabit a world in which any of our individual actions—what we buy, what we eat, what news we share, what we throw away—affect everything else.

Even though we're all existentially connected, each one of us experiences the world through our own eyes, our own filters, and our own emotions.

"A human being is a part of the whole called by us 'Universe,' a part limited in time and space. He experiences himself, his thoughts and feelings as something separated from the rest—a kind of optical delusion of his consciousness.

This delusion is a kind of prison for us, restricting us to our personal desires and to affection for a few persons nearest to us. Our task must be to free ourselves from this prison by widening our circle of compassion to embrace all living creatures and the whole of nature in its beauty."

– ALBERT EINSTEIN

Every one of us has a place. We all have a role to play. Most of us want to make the world a better place for ourselves, our neighbors, and our children.

In some shape or form, we all want to be part of something bigger than ourselves.

We all want to belong.

"Our deepest emotional need is to feel a sense of belonging and significance."

– ALFRED ADLER

CTIVIST. PARENT. T ACHER. CONS
R. NEIGHBOR. FOUNDER. ARTIST.
LUENCER. OFFICIAL. SOCIAL WOF
EADER. FOLLOWER. COUSIN. SIST
EPHEW. NAY-SAYER. PLAYER. OPT
ACIFIST. TEAMMATE. CEO. LABOR
AN. BELIEVER. BROTHER. STEP MC
IRD WATCHER. WHALE WATCHER
NTHUSIAST. CRAFT BEER LOVER.
EE MANIAC. CASUAL GARDENER.
OVA. SERIAL DATER. RECLUSE. FI/
USINESS PARTNER. NEWLYWED. V
NDER. INSOMNIAC. ROCKER. PIAN
INGER-SONGWRITER. NOVELIST.
ATE BLOOMER. PUNK. EARLY RISE
DOPTER. DIGITAL NATIVE. PREPPI
TALLY CHALLENGED. SMART ALEC
LANKET. PESSIMIST. BROWN NOS
ER. RULE BREAKER. PEACE MAKE
EPENDENT. AMATEUR. INTROVERT

And *belonging* is what
this book is about.

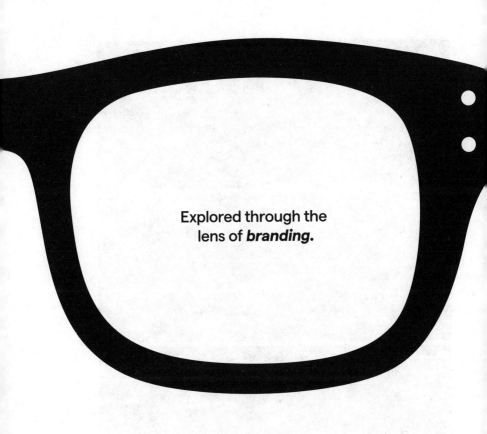

Explored through the
lens of *branding.*

This journey is composed of three parts.

Act 1.

Act 2.

Act 3.

This Is Our Water

In which we explore our current condition, the shaping of our identities, and how their public performance leads us to use tools of branding.

Navigating the Human Zoo

In which we examine human communication and the role symbols and language play in our collaboration and inherent desire for belonging.

Go Humans

In which we challenge ourselves to rediscover a sense of belonging to each other and use branding as a tool that helps us create a shared sense of the threats and opportunities we face—together.

Act 1.

Bathing in Brands

This Is Our
Water

~~~~~~~

There are many unmistakable qualities that unite all human beings.

Some of these qualities lie below the surface. These are things we share and things we do that we are not necessarily aware of.

It can often be difficult to swim against the currents while trying to stay on top of all the stuff that life requires of us. We simply lack the perspective to properly assess what's going on around us.

So what is this liquid we're all swimming in?

– Parable by
DAVID FOSTER WALLACE

Branding & Brands©
Branding & Brands™
Branding & Brands®

Branding
& Brands©
WTF?

You ask?
What are you talking about?
What is the difference?
Isn't branding all about selling stuff?

Sure, most brands want to get as many people as possible to exchange some kind of currency for some sort of good.

However, the act of branding today has little to do with the act of selling.

→ **Branding is the process of distilling something* down to its essence and giving it physical shape.**

*Usually a product, place, service, or person.

Branding used to be about **ownership**—about what belongs <u>to us.</u>

Paintings in Egyptian tombs suggest the origins of branding livestock date back to 2700 BCE. Long before Hernán Cortés brought the idea of branding from Spain to the New World, ancient Greeks and Romans marked their livestock with scorching irons.

(Vintage Cattle Brand Symbols)

BAR O

CROSS AND CRESCENT

LAZY M

ROCKING R

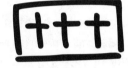

THREE CROSSES

BAR T

PITCHFORK

QUARTER CIRCLE O

TUMBLING T

*Branding was about marking
one's possessions in public.*

The moment the first sizzling iron violently, dramatically, cinematically burned skin, flesh, and fur, human history was forever changed.

By burning a symbol onto another being—a squarely strange act—we had somehow found a way to our ego's heart, awakening a sleeping giant.

While surely not the first time satisfaction was found in the power of amassing material possessions, it helped shape a way of viewing the world through a material lens and paved the way for capitalism to start wrapping its fingers around many of our societies.

Do we belong more when we have more?

As humans moved past crafting individual goods into mass-produced ones, it was essential to stamp a symbol onto a product in order to distinguish one manufacturer from the next.

THESE WERE MANIFESTATIONS OF QUALITY, HERITAGE, AND DIFFERENTIATION.

At some point, we discovered that the purchase, use, or consumption of a product could serve as a reflection of our worldview—our status.

Caviar.
Beaver Hats.
The Automobile.
Fur Coats.
Champagne.

We have gone from wearing pelts for survival to wearing pelts for status.

Attaching value to actions and the consciously public display of labels allows us to seek out the like-minded. The same class. The same wealth. The same team.

Our people. Where we belong.

Was this the moment we surrendered to the brand?

Today, we have no shared mass religion.
We have no more shared mythology.
All of that is forever fragmented.

All of that is history.

Now, we have <u>brands</u>!

brands brands brands

brands brands brands

brands brands brands

brands brands brands

brands brands brands

brands brands brands

Brands are the gods and the titans, the heroes and the villains.

At times benevolent, at times amoral, and at all times self-serving, brands are at the heart of our conflicts and connections. They continue to inspire us, and sometimes they deliver on our greatest hopes.

Brands, much like entertainers, reside in the public sphere. They have to be recognized, believed, adored, followed, and purchased. It is their duty to perform their existence for everyone to see.

Otherwise, they're just another thing in the universe — a tree falling in the forest with no one around to hear it.

In the 80s and 90s, Coke and Pepsi began battling for supremacy in the marketplace.

The efforts ramped up, each brand trying to outdo the other with commercial spectacle and celebrity brand ambassadors.

The battle continues to this day.

The brand is the most ubiquitous and influential entity of our time. First amplified by print and radio, then television, and now social media and mobile devices, the power, reach, pervasiveness, and penetration of brands into our lives is simply immeasurable.

Whether we realize it or not, brands influence the formation of our personal identities, how we relate to one another, what we notice, and what we value. They are present in many of the experiences we have, both public and private. They are woven into our daily interactions, into the deepest fibers of our social fabric, knitting fellow humans together one minute and splitting us into rival tribes the next.

Brands are the ultimate gatekeepers, trendsetters, and mass mind-shapers. They determine who and what we love, who and what we hate, what gets visibility, and what gets marginalized and buried.

Brands are the foundation of the attention economy; without them, we wouldn't be debating how much information the human species can realistically process. We wouldn't be deliberating about how to divide our attention between all the things that require it.

Without brands, we would be hopelessly lost.

Without brands, would we be free?

Branding≠ Marketing

Branding shapes. Marketing <u>sells.</u>

And yes. There is a gray zone — because the shape is essential to the sale.

Branding

Think of branding as _expressing yourself_.

What do you wear to a job interview? A suit?
A dress? Do you want to appear professional or
casual? Sneakers? Heels? Perfume? Cologne?
Do you shave? Put on makeup? What kind of
lipstick? Red? Burgundy? Gloss?

Marketing

Think of marketing as _making your case_.

Why me? How do I fit into the organization?
What's my experience? How do I make your life
better? Easier? How can I help you? What can
I learn from you? What can you learn from me?

Without a doubt, it is getting more and more difficult to distinguish between these two disciplines.

The way I see it, brands need marketing the way fish need water. Without marketing, brands simply cannot navigate the sea of eyeballs needed for survival.

Yes, marketing has changed the world. Billboards alter our skylines, and commercials disrupt our entertainment experiences. But it is not marketing that shapes humanity in such fundamental ways.

It is brands. Like it or not.

Brands
define who
we are.

Brands mark our status, signify our value, and let us broadcast to the world:

"This is who I am."

Consciously, unconsciously—possibly in permanent denial—we are living in a mega-branded reality in which the gestures, messages, imagery, and actions of brands influence us more than we realize.

They touch every facet of human life.

Who are you?
(Really.)

ALE. FEMALE. INTERSEX. TRANSG
AL. QUEER. PANSEXUAL. NON-BIN
ACK. WHITE. BIRACIAL. LATINX.
LE CLASS. WHITE COLLAR. BLUE
EACHER. ACTIVIST. CONFORMIST.
STER.   BEL. A
ENDENT.   R. APOL
RT. EXTR   AL. INTUIT
RESSIVE. R   RELIGIOUS
JNK. EMO. S   AN. HIPPIE. R
IRL. VISIONAR   ACEMAKER. PF
R. LOVER. HATE   TEAM PLAYER. I
OR. LEADER. FOLLOWER. WORLD-
ARTHLING. OTHER. LIBERTARIAN.
OTHER. MULATTO. BUSSER. PATR
AN. STEPBROTHER. PSYCHOLOGI
USTRIALIST. DIGITAL NATIVE. MILL
UTOCRAT. PLUTOCRAT. WARMON
ENDENT. REAGANITE. SOCIALITE.
LASS. EUROPEAN. AMERICAN. AS

The labels we put on each other project a
picture into somebody else's mind.

DER. GAY. BISEXUAL. STRAIGHT. A
Y. GENDER FLUID. QUESTIONING. I
AN. INDIGENOUS. RICH. POOR. MI
LAR. PACIFIST. PATRIOT. SOLDIER
N-CONFORMING. MOTHER. FATH
ETE. LIBERAL. CONSERVATIVE. IN
AL. PROFESSIONAL. AMATEUR. IN
. RULE MAKER. RULE BREAKER. PI
THEIST. AGNOSTIC. AUTHENTIC. G
NECK. PREPPIE. JOCK. TOMBOY. G
MATIST. CONTRARIAN. WINNER.
NOCLAST. ARTIST. DREAMER. INV
ANGER. AMERICAN. GLOBAL CITI
HEW. GRANDFATHER. GREAT-GR
NURSE. MINER. DESIGNER. ZOOF
NATIONALIST. PACIFIST. ARTIST. I
NIAL. NARCISSIST. LIAR. DEMOCR
R. PEACEMAKER. INDEPENDENT. D
D DIGGER. UPPER CLASS. WORK
PROFESSIONAL. AMATEUR. PLAY

YOU ARE MORE THAN YOUR

Branded
Shit!

YOU ARE MORE THAN A LABEL

Still, these labels reflect and reinforce aspects of you.
The way you see yourself. The way others see you.
The way you wish you were. The way you'll never be.
And what you really are.

We're all caught between fantasy and reality.

Is everything around us an illusion?

Brands help us create illusions of ourselves.

A trove of psychological studies suggest a connection between positive self-perception and well-being.

This makes sense: When we feel good internally, we are more competent and socially confident. We tend to be more helpful and cooperative. We are better problem solvers. We are motivated to succeed and more likely to persist in the face of challenges.

Our self-perception, however, is not always on point. We can easily be deluded, overestimate our abilities or our capacity to be objective, or fall prey to peer pressure, unconscious bias, or outside manipulation.

And yes, brands can feed and play on these delusions and prejudices.

Yet, brands also have a way of teasing out the best in us. They help us feel attractive, prosperous, and together. They make us feel part of a group, like we belong. They help us maintain optimism about ourselves and the world. Whether it's a flashy new pair of kicks, a new car, or a motivating app, brands can dramatically alter our moods, our energy levels, and how we see ourselves.

This power is a double-edged sword.

It is to our benefit that we're drawn to offerings that help us thrive, succeed, understand ourselves better, and achieve more happiness.

But are we just flaunting what we've got? Living a life of empty materialism and compensating for our insecurities? Or are the brands in our lives serving a deeper purpose, supporting our best possible selves, our strongest relationships, our most viable society?

While surely less dramatic and painful than a sizzling iron, each one of us is stamped from our beginnings.

We are assigned a sex, skin color, and nationality that give us permission to exist in one tiny, specific sliver of this universe.

Only later in life, when we are of "legal age," do a few narrow choices open up for us. Immigration and sexual identity, are, however, not even playing fields. It depends on where you're from, what you do, and whether your personal wealth allows you to choose where you want to belong to.

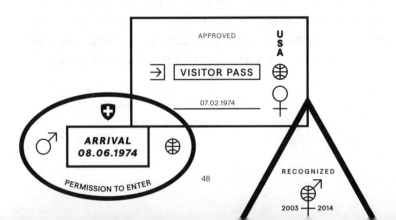

48

If America is a nation of immigrants, how does one become American?

A passport might be the most tangible representation —the physical proof—of our belonging to a certain tribe. It allows us to cross our invented borders—or be rejected by them.

It is, however, the _intangible_ aspects of citizenship that often have the most impact on our sense of kinship.

The rituals.
The pledges.
The anthems.

The stories.

Yes, branding is a process.

Branding ≠ Brand

BRANDING
2003 — 2014

MADE IN USA

★ ★ ★

BRANDED

Oct 15 | 12

Our public discourse tends to live in a gray zone; terms are used interchangeably, definitions glossed over, and specificity generalized. And most of the time, these "language sketches" work perfectly fine.

Branding and _brand_ are terms that live in that gray zone and often get thrown into one bucket.

In my mind, there is, however, a clear distinction:

Branding is the _process_ that leads to the brand.

And yes, branding is much bigger than brands.

BRANDING IS A

54

All of us use it.

Most use it in <u>public</u>.
Many use it for <u>profit.</u>
Some use it for <u>power.</u>

It is rarely used in private.

Who am I?

"This is how I dress. This is how I speak. This is what I do. This is how I play. This is how I pray. This is who I love. This is what I believe."

"This is who I am."

This is what branding does.

At some point in our evolution as individual humans, we become aware of how our appearance, our actions, or the way we communicate affects our surroundings.

And once we start to consciously shape **_appearance_**, **_messaging_**, and **_behavior_**, we apply tools of branding.

April 17 / 2015

However, none of us act—or perform—the same way in every social setting, for every audience.

Most of us display one version of ourselves when we visit our family and another one when we hang out with our friends. Sitting across the table from a stranger tends to lead to a different performance than approaching an acquaintance.

Our role as a parent is separate from that of a presenter in a professional setting. And parenting at home will most likely differ in performance from parenting at a public playground.

"Choose your self-presentations carefully, for what starts out as a mask may become your face."

– ERVING GOFFMAN

An audience of one is much more intimate than an audience of many. And the audience of a few is far more personal than an audience of the masses.

Which version of us—is us?

We have never had this many ways to express ourselves.

As society advances—sometimes fast, more often agonizingly slow—through stage upon stage of cultural evolution, it tends to grow more tolerant of lifestyles and expressions that may have been frowned upon at some point in time.

Physically, we have endless fashion choices, a vast array of cosmetics, body modification options, and accessories to shape the identity of our wildest dreams.

Blogs and social media platforms give each of us a voice and the ability to share anything with the world, from curated pictures of our homes and snapshots of our vacations to what we're reading, what we had for breakfast, or whatever it is that inspires us and makes us think:

Y'all need to see this!

On top of that, we have virtually unlimited tools to create art, music, and visual content. These tools, once accessible only to professionals, have now been democratized like never before.

In the hands of digital natives, these tools are shaping what we see, watch, read, and hear. In inspirational ways. In transformative ways. In overwhelming ways.

Deepfakes on Facebook are coming.

Infants are already born on Instagram.

And memes have become the conventional form of memorializing shared events.

CRAY CRAY!

Yes, it's a little crazy. Maybe a little scary.

But while there have never been this many ways to conceal ourselves and deceive one another, there have also never been so many ways to actively shape and communicate such specific, diverse, and fully realized versions of ourselves.

In the past, society dictated who we were, who we could be, and what roles we would play in the world. And, objectively, those roles were pretty narrow.

But now, we have control.*

If you live in the right state, country, community.

Now, we have the power to choose.

We have the power to create our identities, instead of passively accepting pre-established ones. With that opportunity comes immense potential for creativity, self-transformation, and societal change.

As we strive to define and differentiate ourselves in this complicated world, brands become unmatched tools of self-definition.

While some brands are simply stamped upon us—Swiss, American, Japanese—most other brands enrich who we are, revealing vital details about us wherever we go.

Above all, they give us a niche, a way, and a place to belong.

Now, we need the strength to remain ourselves.

Because the flip side of this proverbial coin is that there are more pressures on us to look a certain way, buy a certain thing, and belong to a certain group.

Entertainment.

News.

Advertising.

Social Media.

You are
what you
eat.

And more often than not, we are eating alone.

Long before information became "snackable" and paragraphs became pictures, food became "fast." Designed to keep us going rather than keep us nourished, fast food has become the premium fuel of postmodern capitalism.

Convenient? Certainly.

Yet it robs us all of one of the few opportunities for connection a shared meal provides.

The same is true for information. Communal evening news has been replaced with headlines pushed to our personal devices, all day, every day. Curiosity-based inquiry has been substituted with unsolicited "news flashes" from various media brands.

This lack of critical sounding boards leaves us eating, thinking, and digesting alone through much of our lives.

They say not all those who wander are lost, but I'm the only one out here and idk, the sun is going down and it's getting kinda sketchy so I might not fit that description.

A table for one, please.

Ladies and gentlemen, welcome to the void!

Even before the global pandemic of 2020, jobs were lost in many industries across many economies. As the world went into lockdown to defeat the virus, human labor was further reduced for health reasons.

All of this has exposed many more existing cracks in many more of our structures than many of us anticipated. Some of the cracks have even expanded.

Wider. Deeper.

This is a potentially explosive environment.

Sickness, poverty, and a lack of the purpose that honest work provides can lead to social unrest and populist revolutions. People turn against each other, against their government, against authority figures. They want to tear down the system that has left them without opportunity.

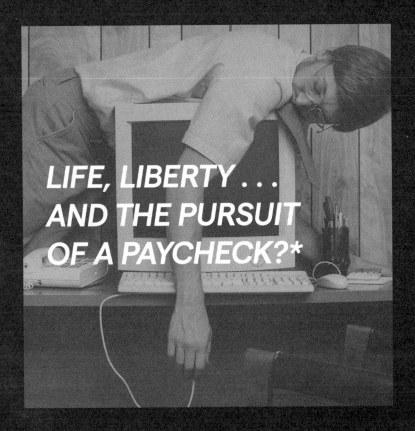

LIFE, LIBERTY . . . AND THE PURSUIT OF A PAYCHECK?*

EACHER. CEO. WELDER. DENTIST.
LUENCER. MARKETING GURU. SC
EPORTER. POLICE OFFICER. PROG
ECEPTIONIST. STOCK TRADER. HO
RUCK DRIVER. COMEDIAN. ~~STORE~~
~~OTANIST.~~ POLITICIAN. DOG WALK
T. CINEMATOGRAPHER. SALESPEI
IAL AGENT. VETERINARIAN. MENT
OACH. EDITOR. DESIGNER. RESEA
ST. ~~TECHNICIAN~~. PHYSICIST. CHIL
NE WORKER. SECRETARY. ACTOR
EADER. ANIMAL ~~RESCUER.~~ AESTH
AKER. ANTHROPOLOGIST. MASSE
ORKER. DANCER. EVENT PLANNE
CE REP. COUSIN. COMMUNITY LE
NTREPRENEUR. CHANGEMAKER. E
ALESMAN. CEO. ~~CMO.~~ PASTOR. CO
HEF. SURGEON. PSYCHOTHERAPIS
R. ~~BUS DRIVER.~~ STOCK BROCKER.
OPY EDITOR. HR PROFESSIONAL.

CTOR. LAWYER. CHEF. NURSE. IN
TIST. WRITER. SOLDIER. POLITICIA
MMER. ~~ARCHITECT.~~ ACCOUNTAN
E TRAINER. SECURITY GUARD. MA
~~ERK.~~ BANKER. STRATEGIST. MUSI
~~MECHANIC.~~ BUSINESS OWNER. A
N. ACTIVIST. NANNY. INVENTOR.
BUILDER. MANAGER. ARCHEOLO
HER. COUNSELOR. MASSAGE THE
DVOCATE. PRO ATHLETE. ASSEM
CIAL MEDIA MANAGER. RELIGIO
CIAN. ~~ENGINEER.~~ PHOTOGRAPHE
. ~~POSTAL WORKER.~~ CONSTRUCT
MACHINE OPERATOR. CUSTOMER
ER. MOM. DAD. DIPLOMAT. EXECU
CATOR. ~~SOCIAL WORKER.~~ USED
PREACHER. ~~SECURITY GUARD.~~ PA
LANDSCAPE DESIGNER. TELEMAR
AL ESTATE AGENT. JANITOR. CELL
RSE. ASSISTANT. ENTREPRENEUR.

YOU'LL NEVER WALK ALONE

L.F.C.

LIVERPOOL FC

Clubs, for brief and fleeting moments in time, have the power to transcend label and class.

We are linked. But are we connected?

Teams of all stripes—sports teams, book clubs, bands, sororities, neighborhoods—connect some of us while keeping others out. This is the consequence of branding: *it creates _in-groups_ and _out-groups_.*

Seeking to build on our emotional connections, we have physically connected our communities through concrete and cables.

Yet we still often roam alone, protected by branded aluminum and a bubble wrap of information. In the spirit of progress, we have built our modern lifestyles around systems that link us but don't necessarily connect us.

Which goes against the core of our existence.

Deep in our hearts, in the core of our limbic brains, we belong to a herd; we are tribal, communal, social.

We cannot thrive alone.

Even if we think we enjoy solitude, the belief that we can survive alone is mostly an illusion.

Technically it's possible, but it's a lot easier when you can depend on other people to help you out, provide daily services, and make all the stuff you'd never be able to make for yourself.

This is the benefit of living in a society.

The price is, well, other people.

This is the challenge of getting along, the challenge of understanding one another and agreeing on things. This could be a Facebook debate about politics (with people you haven't seen since high school), seeing eye to eye with your neighbor on your property line, or politicians meeting halfway on fiscal policy.

And most of us—even those who are not that social or dislike some of the baggage that comes with being connected to others—relish it when people notice us, are friendly and approving.

Ironically, the devices that are meant to connect us keep us isolated from one another and sheltered in our own information echo chambers.

Yet, the others are not invading our world.
They're sharing it.

They believe what you don't believe.*

Religion has become, in many cases, a parody of itself, exposed as corrupt or simply irrelevant to a growing number of people.

Marketers have labeled different generations as if they are entirely different species from one another.

*Does it matter?

Boomers.
Gen X.
Millennials.
Gen Z.

Welcome to the Brand Industrial Complex.

Our once shared mass culture—*movies, music, art, news channels, novels, TV networks*—has broken into a billion pieces, leaving us adrift in a sea of limitless choices—an omnichannel of dubious information—and creatively bankrupt glut.

Like hungry rats in a maze, we navigate ads, content, feeds, and games, only to find empty rewards at every other turn. We spend endless hours disconnected from life and each other as scientists and algorithms subtly manipulate our behavior and perception to a degree we are only just beginning to comprehend.

PEAK EVERYTHING PEAK EVERYTHING PEAK EVERYTHING PEAK EVERYTHING

As we move toward peak individuality, we are also approaching peak homogenization and peak connectivity at peak technological speed.

Industrial production pushes to increase returns, growth, and yields in all areas—from agriculture and investment to fast fashion, music, art, and publishing. That process commodifies cultural movements and decimates unique biodiversity.

We are approaching global monoculture.

Even events that once brought us together now fail to achieve significant social cohesion, while potent drivers of polarization have gained strength and momentum.

There are a record number of people on the planet—
with no consensus reality.

And, as we fight to "be ourselves," exploring, trying on
nuanced and complex personal identities, we don't
see that only one thing truly unites us all, across all
barriers and categories: *that we are rushing, as one
herd, to the brink of extinction.*

"[. . .] what if we've hit the limit of our capacity to
get along? [. . .] Are we capable as a species of
coordinating our actions at a scale necessary
to address the most dire problems we face?"

– FARHAD MANJOO / The New York Times

We are all migrants now, dislocated in history, endlessly consuming fragments of every culture that ever existed.

Rapidly outgrowing old paradigms, we are blurring all lines and breaking down all border walls. We continue to clutch at categories, even as they limit us, divide us, and tribalize us.

We continue to search—to know ourselves, to find our niche—because we all start off lost and wandering, hungry for meaning and belonging.

Where do you belong?

We swim in this gray space called reality, in which we often can't see past our tiring arms.

The things that happen around us, if observed with objectivity, don't necessarily have to be the cause of disagreement. However, media filters and brand agendas make us see the world in entirely different ways, as if we were living on different planets.

And yet we buy the same sneakers, the same cars, the same devices. We share many tangible ways we live our lives.

Brands connect us, just as they drive us apart.

"Republicans buy sneakers too."

– MICHAEL JORDAN

BRANDED WE RISE.
BRANDED WE FALL.

We are overwhelmed and overworked. Everything around us seems overhyped, which leaves us over-stimulated.

We overspend. We overeat. Some of us overdose, tragically. The internet leads us to be overinformed yet uneducated most of the time.

The world is overpopulated.

Many of us overanalyze and overthink. We regularly work overtime and overdraft our bank accounts.

Anybody else over this?

Are we hopelessly, forever f*cked?

This question is reasonable. It is a logical response to our lived reality. But that doesn't mean our feelings are accurate or that our perceptions of the moment are going to determine the future of our species.

The average person is trying to survive the grind while navigating a sea of endless distractions. It's not hard to explain why many of us mentally check out.

We seem to be struggling to cope with loneliness and social atomization. We're not free enough or secure enough to think about the future or assess reality in a big-picture way.

All over the world, on every continent, in every culture, we seem to overpromise and underdeliver.

We undervalue others. We underestimate our capacity to enact change. We are helplessly underprepared for the havoc we've inflicted on our planet.

We underfund almost everything that could support the underprivileged: healthcare, education, and infra- structure.

Not all of this is necessarily done with mal-intent. It is the result of the systems we have built, tilted in favor of the upper class from the very beginning.

Yet a great deal of it is regularly done with purpose in order to maximize profits, with blatant disregard for people, planet, and politics.

Global plutocrats, corporate leaders, and oligarchs are planning for the future—for the projected hazards they anticipate, even for how they can profit from the spoils of disaster capitalism once the crises hit critical mass.

Brands fuel this world we live in.

They finance our TV shows, our sports teams, our scientific research, and our cultural institutions.

They even pay our politicians—sometimes secretly, sometimes purposely in the open.

But, regardless of whether they savor the spotlight or prefer the shadows backstage, they're ever-present, holding our capitalist system together like mortar fusing bricks. Like a loyal pet, they doggedly follow us around in our browsers and mobile apps, patiently begging for that next click.

EST. 1998

What's wrong with that?

Well, nothing really. The contribution of brands to our cultural fabric is immeasurable.

It becomes convoluted when political donations are made to influence policy, taxes, and regulations. And corporate profits—profits made by promoting goods in the public sphere, using public infrastructure—are allowed to be hidden and withheld from contribution to the public good, benefitting only a select few at the top of the food chain.

It gets even more complex when brands make profits without consent from the customer.

Our reality has been hacked for profit.

Facebook is the real-life Matrix we live in. The digital set of the Truman Show.

Once hailed as an innovation of limitless potential for the future of tech-fueled democracy, for fulfilling the human need of belonging, it has become awash with such a vast amount of disinformation—domestic, foreign, stateless—it is tearing reality to shreds every minute it continues to operate in this manner.

Sadly, it has become a near-religious experience for many of us to scroll our way to salvation without recognizing that it leaves us floating in digital spacetime, untethered from truth, unlinked from reality.

Welcome to the Book of Morons.

*THE BOOK

MORPHEUS

T~~he Matri~~x is everywhere, it is all
around us. Even now, in this very
room. You can see it when you look out
your window, or when you turn on your
television. You can feel it when you go
to work, or when you go to church or when
you pay your taxes. It is the world that
has been pulled over your eyes to blind
you from the truth.

NEO

What truth?

MORPHEUS

That you are a slave. Like everyone
else, you were born into bondage, born
inside a prison that you cannot smell,
taste, or touch. A prison for your mind.
Unfortunately, no one can be told what
*~~The Matrix~~ is. You have to see it for
yourself. This is your last chance.
After this, there is no turning back.

– Excerpt from THE MATRIX
by **LILLY & LANA WACHOWSKI**

When we are adrift, we have anchors of the most ancient and authentic sort available to us, however disguised or distorted they may appear in our lives.

When we are lost, in the midst of chaos, we need symbols and stories, including the ones brands tell, to ground us and root us.

In our fragmented, postmodern condition, we drift toward forces and figures that orient us, that give us practical definitions and the tools to form a coherent worldview of what we stand for or to signify what we belong to—whether it's right or wrong.

Diluted—even perverted—as the symbols, messages, and stories in our landscape may be, brands provide useful fictions, aspirational images, and simple, emotionally resonant narratives that help us grasp our reality—or augment it to our liking.

However, that reality has become increasingly and overwhelmingly complex.

Are there simply too many stories to keep us connected?

Therefore, to really comprehend what's going on around us, what is happening to us, and how we might steer our way out of the confusion, we have to look back.

Way back.

We have to take a broader view.

In order to regain our humanity and our respect for fellow humans, we have to examine what defines our humanness.

In order to resolve our longing for belonging, we must revisit our origins and retrace our steps.

Act 2.

Language, Label, and Symbol

Navigating the Human Zoo

Earth.
Rock.
Light.
Shadow.
Fire.
Myths.
Stories.
Symbols.
Shelter.

First home.
First canvas.
First sanctuary.

First theater of the mind.

First circle of belonging.

This cave is where our story begins, the natural shelter we inhabited before we made our own.

This is the birthplace of art.
This is the accelerator of language.
This is the first workshop, with tools of fire and stone.

This is the theater where our earliest stories, dramas, and myths were told and shaped, the first place we could call our own—as a home, as a sacred space.

This is the first place we gathered as families, as clans.

This is where we were safe to survive—together.

The cave was the first extension of the mind.

The pigment is the first letter in this story.

Discovered as a tool to represent the physical world, it was used to record our surroundings, from animals to trees to stories of successful hunting excursions.

Over time, these forms evolved into symbols less descriptive in shape yet more refined in meaning.

This evolution takes us all the way to the printing press and—more recently—to the pixels that make up our modern screens. This process is still taking shape today. The purpose, however, remains the same: coping with and communicating about a changing and unpredictable world.

This is the dawn of civilization.

In prehistoric times, we lived in small tribal bands, isolated from our neighbors, encountering outsiders infrequently. Back then, our local hunting grounds were the entire world. Our people, our language, our rituals, our myths, and our creation stories were the only ones we ever had to be concerned with.

There is harmony in homogeneity. Communication feels natural. Cooperation comes easier. Historical observations of egalitarianism, generosity, and social cohesion among indigenous peoples, prior to colonial interference, depict this.

That isn't to say the prehistoric world was without conflict. But lower population density and healthy distance between groups naturally reduced the likelihood of violent interactions.

We simply had no idea how big the world truly was, how many other humans were out there, or how much there was to compete over.

There was no concept of property, nations, or borders. And no maps to manifest those separations. We had only primitive tools and clothes, and few valuable possessions others might covet. We did not even have many cultural distinctions; archaeological records show that no matter where people lived, they lived pretty much the same—very crudely.

Much of what generates conflict and competition between groups simply didn't yet exist.

And our symbols were still mostly simple, positive representations of that life.

There is no disputing that thought, dreams, language, art, rituals, music, human imagination, the urge to worship—the innate impulse to create anything at all—have always been deeply intertwined.

Through every age of human experience, we reach ever new levels of sophistication. Stage by violent and glorious stage, consciousness evolves. And as a result, our way of living changes, our technology advances, and how we see ourselves and how we relate to others evolves.

But we have not embarked on this journey alone.

Alongside us—arising, multiplying, undergoing endless adaptations—are our stories and symbols.

We shape them, and they shape us in return.

"Fiction has enabled us not merely to imagine things, but to do so collectively. [. . .] Any large-scale human cooperation—whether a modern state, a medieval church, an ancient city, or an archaic tribe—is rooted in common myths that exist only in people's collective imagination."

– YUVAL NOAH HARARI / SAPIENS

Let's consider this.

Whether it's leaning on the Ten Commandments to instill ethical behavior in society, fueling a revolt over excessive taxation, or using the myth of William Tell to lay the foundation of the future Swiss state—these are stories that gain their power only by masses of people believing them enough to affect their actions.

The power of the story is remarkable.

"There are no gods, no nations, no money and no human rights, except in our collective imagination."

– YUVAL NOAH HARARI / SAPIENS

It is that imagination, combined with our inherent curiosity, that has driven us out of the cave.

Down the hill.
Across the plains.
Over the mountain pass.

As we continued to push the edge of the known world outward, humans had to find a way to trust the information they received from those selected to find out what's in the next valley, behind the distant mountain, across the shore of the lake.

And yes, of course there were doubters.

And explorers across time were questioned, ridiculed, and imprisoned—or worse, burned at the stake.

EDGE OF THE SOLAR SYSTEM
EDGE OF THE PLANET
EDGE OF THE CONTINENT
EDGE OF THE TERRITORY
EDGE OF THE VALLEY
EDGE OF THE FOREST

This is the dawn of communication.

There are three fundamentally different ways human beings communicate with each other.

Verbal and gestural communication require rather close contact. After we speak, after we send a signal through our movement, our hands, our actions—after information is transmitted—the message is gone for the rest of eternity, except in the minds and hearts of other human beings.

Of the three, graphic communication is the only form that is transmitted and preserved beyond a single moment in time.*

This is the start of the recording of information and the verification of data.

* **GENEVIEVE VON PETZINGER**
TED Talk

VERBAL

GESTURAL

GRAPHIC

(Geometric Signs of Ice Age Europe)

ASTERISK

AVIFORM

CIRCLE

CORDIFORM

CROSSHATCH

CRUCIFORM

HALF CIRCLE

OPEN ANGLE

OVAL

PECTIFORM

SCLARIFORM

ZIGZAG

* GENEVIEVE VON PETZINGER
TED Talk

Most species have the ability to communicate with each other in some shape or form.

What separates graphic communication from its verbal and gestural cousins is that it allows societies to record information with greater detail and more consistency than by spoken word alone. It allows for the transmission of information and the preservation of knowledge for future generations.

For the story of humans, graphic symbols change everything.

It is believed some of the first messages between humans weren't actually writing as we know it. They could have been gestures or tokens: a flower outside someone's hut as a symbol of tenderness, a pile of rocks along a trail warning of danger.*

Over time, these messages evolved into graphic symbols. This was the beginning of alphabets.

* Examples from fonts.com

PHOENICIAN ALEF

EGYPTIAN HIEROGLYPH

PHOENICIAN GIMEL

GREEK ALPHA

PHOENICIAN BETH

EARLY GREEK LETTER

LATER GREEK ALPHA

EARLY GREEK BETA

LATER GREEK LETTER

ROMAN AH

LATER GREEK BETA

ROMAN LETTER

For every mark to be recognized and remembered, each for its singular meaning, it had to be simple and well crafted. From the very beginning, writing was an art form.

However, just like a single human, a single letterform is rather useless.

It is only by connecting individual letters to each other in the right order and orientation that we arrive at the written language we know from books and newspapers. It allows us to connect different ideas and transfer thoughts from our brains to sand on a beach, sheets of paper, or, now, pixels on a screen.

That language is only useful if there are other humans to communicate with—an audience for our hopes, dreams, complaints, and fears.

Word

Sentence

Paragraph

Chapter

Story

"Language is the instrument of thought."

– NOAM CHOMSKY / The Ezra Klein Show

We are linked through language.

Deep in our brains, we are hardwired to express ourselves, to share our lives and stories with fellow members of our tribes.

We cannot thrive alone.

Shared communication bonds individuals to a society through a shared sense of the world. It allows us to comfort each other. It allows for collaboration, from communal hunting and agriculture to rituals and self-governance. And the recording of rules and laws. It affirms a sense of belonging to our fellow humans.

Among those who speak the same language.

Language is what separates us from other beings.
It gives form to the first sounds we utter.

Language shapes vows and eulogies. It paints worlds in literature and pens stories for cinema.

It lays out global treaties. It delivers declarations of peace, love, and war.

While most people can read those declarations and write more or less coherently about them—willingly or unwillingly—there are some of us who can't.

For people who are unable to communicate through written or spoken words, most notably the blind and the deaf-mute, we have developed alternative means of delivering and receiving information.

While sign language relies on hand gestures to shape letters, words, feelings, and actions, braille converts the traditional alphabet into graphic arrangements and dimensional patterns.

yes

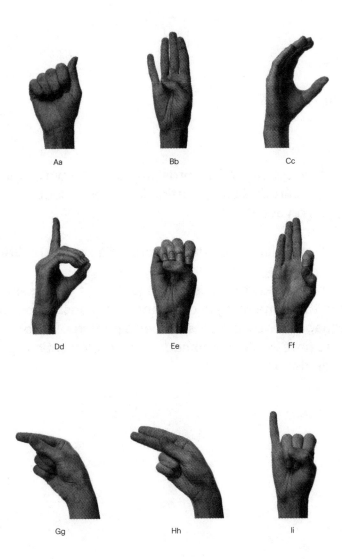

Aa   Bb   Cc

Dd   Ee   Ff

Gg   Hh   Ii

When we speak—with words or gestures—we shape the world around us by putting labels on objects, on people, on events.

It is through language that we create a shared reality.

However, words for the same object don't necessarily mean the same thing in different languages. Some languages have no words for certain things, while others have acutely nuanced ways of differentiating one single thing.

Some people see beauty in the world.
Others, only despair. Which one is real?

Plate

Lampshade

Cup

Candle

Flowers

Knob

Drawer

Pillow

Chair

China

Chest

Ceci n'est pas une pomme.

This is not an apple.

Language, describing objects

Among the components of _structural linguistics_ is the arbitrariness of words assigned to objects and the relationship between sign, signifier, and signified.

Sign

The sign is the _actual object_ in question.

Signifier

This refers to the _physical existence_ of any object: the sound, the word, or the image.

Signified

The signified is the _mental concept_ of the object: fruit, freshness, temptation, fertility, health, etc.

This is how we construct our world.

Even though we're all composed of the same basic material, we all have different ways of processing our physical world. And if we were in charge of writing our story, we would all write different versions.

In addition to providing us with the instrument to label our objects, language helps us articulate our emotions and describe our actions for the people around us, for the people who will come after us.

Language is what preserves human history. In many ways, language is what shapes our history, because it depends on who puts which words on paper and what is left out, by accident or intention.

"He who controls the past commands the future.
He who commands the future conquers the past."

– GEORGE ORWELL

And yes, much of our history
has been written by men.

1619

PROJECT

A HISTORY
OF THE UNITED STATES OF AMERICA

★ ★ ★ ★ ★

BY

A PULITZER PRIZE–WINNING BLACK FEMALE REPORTER
COVERING RACIAL INJUSTICE AND WRITERS FROM
THE NEW YORK TIMES AND *NEW YORK TIMES MAGAZINE*

AUGUST 2019

Who is telling the story?

The
1776
Report

A HISTORY
OF THE UNITED STATES OF AMERICA

★ ★ ★ ★ ★

BY

AN 18-MEMBER, MOSTLY WHITE, MOSTLY MALE
COMMISSION OF APPOINTED CONSERVATIVE
ACTIVISTS, POLITICIANS, AND INTELLECTUALS

JANUARY 2021

What is their agenda?

Before we learned to reproduce goods, we had to learn how to reproduce thought. It is that process that made ideas available to the masses.

The invention of the printing press took the audience for human ideas to unprecedented heights. It is the printed word that allowed gospels to spread much greater distances, commerce to connect people from all corners of the globe, and philosophies to lay the foundation for large populations.

Handwriting

Garamond

Bodoni

Futura

Times Roman

Helvetica

Karma

1532

1788

1930

1931

1957

2017

*Fonts give language physical shape.
And, just like language, that shape evolves over time.*

The printing press produced typography.

Typography is the art of arranging individual letters into words, paragraphs, and, ultimately, narratives—making written language legible.

While aesthetic considerations may not be essential to conveying the information itself, the physical shape of the written word can further reinforce the information that is being transmitted.

Typographic tools include the selection of typefaces, type sizes, line length, line spacing *(leading)*, letter spacing *(tracking)*, and adjusting the space between individual letters *(kerning)*.

It is typography that allows us to reproduce language consistently and give it a more stable shape for its journey around the world.

Somehow, putting words through a machine solidifies thoughts more so than simply pen and paper; it allows for more comprehensive refinement and gives writers the means for more efficient editing.

It equips graphic designers with the tools to infuse text with an additional layer of meaning—emotion even. It helps them approximate the tone of spoken words. There are ways to make type feel humorous, official, inviting, loud, oppressive, or quiet.

Typography laid the foundation for brands.

Repetition. Repetition. Repetition is one of the most vital instruments in branding.

Typography and its purposeful, consistent usage by brands—implemented many years after the printing press was introduced—is what makes a product or a service recognizable to their customers.

It is only after corporations recognize the value of a consistent visual identity for themselves—and their products—that typography becomes a tool in the brand toolbox.

It helps establish graphic design as a craft.

Logo of Bass Brewery's Pale Ale from 1876. The oldest trademark registered with the Patent Office (UK) and arguably the oldest trademark in the world.

Typography allows us to shape logotypes, paragraphs, and words.

WRDS. W   S. WORD
. WORDS. WORD   ORDS. WORDS.
JS. WORDS. WORDS. WORDS. WORDS. W
RDS. WORDS. WORDS. WORDS. WORDS. WO
RDS. WORDS. WORDS. WORDS. WORDS. WOF
RDS. WORDS. WORDS. WORDS. WORDS. WOF
RDS. WORDS. WORDS. WORDS. WORDS. WO'
'DS. WORDS. WORDS. WORDS. WORDS. WC
JS. WORDS. WORDS. WORDS. WORDS. W
. WORDS. WORDS. WORDS. WORDS. '
VORDS. WORDS. WORDS. WORDS
RDS. WORDS. WORDS. WOF
S. WORDS. WORDS. W
'ORDS. WORD'
^ V

Words of comfort.

Words of combat.

Words allow us to shape labels.

They are born with our inception—built into the way we communicate and the way we construct our world.

They shape our identities.

And we shape those identities in return. While the majority of us stick to our assigned labels and find a way to inhabit them, there are many who choose to shape their own—be it in name or gender or both.

Labels shape the world, and our place in it.

Bestowed upon us by our tribe, our name is intended to help us fit in—or stand out. With only the best of intentions, it can become a kind of verbal armor—or a heavy chain—for this battle we call life.

The same is true of family histories.

We embellish certain parts and leave out others, consciously crafting public perceptions that fit our individual narratives.

Hallowed be thy name.

For centuries, bloodlines have determined political power structures.

By allowing us to identify the physical world around us, labels help us approach a semblance of a shared reality. On the other hand, they equip us with the tools to segment people into categories.

We stick labels on the others.

We judge members of our tribe, and ourselves.

And often not in the most productive ways.

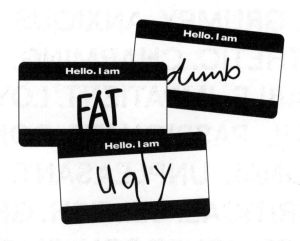

UMB. SMART. TALL. SHORT. BRIGI
UPT. RICH. POOR. PRETTY. UGLY.
ARK. MEAN. NICE. AUTHENTIC. F/
NTIVE. ARTISTIC. BRAVE. CLUMS
RERANT. FRIENDLY. KIND. NUMB. I
ULNERABLE. WARY. UNPOPULAR.
UTSPOKEN. MODEST.
E. HAPPY. AGER. DE
UNT. COOL. GUARDED
UTGOING. QUI UD. RESTLES
TRONG. WARM. COLD. FRIENDLY.
OPULAR. SELFISH. WISE. VAIN. SI
ROUS. GRUMPY. ANXIOUS. BOSSY
YMPATHETIC. CHARMING. DIPLON
DAPTABLE. IMPATIENT. LOYAL. AD
OPEFUL. PASSIONATE. ROMANTI(
MOTIONAL. UNPLEASANT. UNFRII
YPOCRITICAL. SELFISH. GREEDY.
JL. LAZY. STUBBORN. EMOTIONA
REVERENT. OBESE. EXPLOSIVE. N

Language shapes
labels of love.

ENSE. FAT. THIN. ETHICAL. COR-
ISERVATIVE. PROGRESSIVE. LIGH
COLD. HOT. LAZY. AMBITIOUS. A
SRUPTIVE. EAGER. CURIOUS. INT
TE. RESOURCEFUL. SAD. TACTLES
OUGHTFUL. SLOW. SASSY. PENSIV
HARGIC. IMPULSIVE. FLAKY. GEN
TE. CAREFUL. CARELESS. COHER
VESOME. MORONIC. OBNOXIOUS
LLY. TOLERANT. VIGILANT. WEAK
NY. HONEST. Y. POPULAR. L
UTGOING. CALM. GEN
PENDABLE T. RELIABL
C. GIVING. RDWORKI
TUROUS. CHEERFUL. JUDGEMEN
SCHIEVOUS. SARCASTIC. TOUGH
Y. DISOBEDIENT. NASTY. CARELE:
ERABLE. COMMON. PETTY. BEAU
MID. SHORT-TEMPERED. ORDINAI
ISSISTIC. BRASH. MEEK. MORBID

Language
shapes labels of hate.

From language of opportunity . . .

Generation by generation, we have chiseled and molded the way we communicate, which, in turn, has shaped the stories that sustain us.

This is true in literature and in law, in cinema and in culture.

Language is a living, breathing organism—the force that bonds our families, our tribes, our generations.

It shapes stories of beauty and belonging.

> *"Linguistic imperialism is the imposition of one language on speakers of other languages. It is also known as linguistic nationalism, linguistic dominance, and language imperialism. In our time, the global expansion of English has often been cited as the primary example of linguistic imperialism."*
>
> **– RICHARD NORDQUIST** / ThoughtCo.

. . . to language of oppression.

It also shapes stories of venom and violence.

From verbal bullying to harassment, from legitimizing persecution to disseminating propaganda, language can be harmful and dangerous.

A common practice of conquering nations has been to outlaw the religious and ceremonial customs of the conquered. Forcing native people to speak the oppressor's tongue is a further extension of that vicious practice.

On the surface, this is a simple demonstration of power. Underneath, however, it's easy to recognize that linguistic imperialism serves a much larger goal: to enforce a worldview, overriding the existing one.

Language is a barrier.

The withholding of education to keep a segment of a population locked into a certain social status may be one of the more cynical strategies of oppression. It denies people the tools required to climb the social ladder, one of the main "selling points" of Western democracy.

But whatever the cynicism of the tools, rest assured human beings have employed them in some shape or form to serve their agendas.

"It was a criminal act to teach a black person who was enslaved to read [. . .] Black Americans have always understood for literacy to be freedom."

– NIKOLE HANNAH-JONES

From denied access to education to the information design of election ballots, DMV forms, and green card applications, language continues to complicate access to services for certain groups of people.

Of course, not all of it is done with mal-intent.

But every fellow immigrant has probably questioned at one point or another why certain information or processes couldn't be simplified.

Is it fair to wonder whether a stubborn adherence to archaic and inaccessible language for legal purposes has intentionally been preserved to make it harder for people without means to access lawyers and other legal services?

Type the code shown

DENIED

Language is a weapon.

One need look no further than the vitriolic presidency of Donald J. Trump to be reminded of the corrosive power of words.

Other fascist leaders throughout history have likewise used language to demonize and threaten rivals and, in some cases, the state itself.

The verbal attacks, bullying, and vilifying have the same effect on society as sustained aerial strikes in times of war; it is exhausting, leaving the landscape littered with casualties. And the end goal is clear: complete capitulation.

> "[. . .] an expression of a world in which everyone is desperately seeking their own audience and fracturing reality in the process."
>
> **– CHARLIE WARZEL**
> On Michael Goldhaber / The New York Times

"Americans are the great Satan, the wounded snake."

– AYATOLLAH KHOMEINI

"The only white man you can trust is a dead white man."

– ROBERT MUGABE

"Let us have a dagger between our teeth, a bomb in our hands, and an infinite scorn in our hearts."

– BENITO MUSSOLINI

"I do not see why man should not be just as cruel as nature."

– ADOLF HITLER

Are there laws for the use of language?

Apart from rules of grammar and punctuation, which govern the mechanics of language, there are not many other guidelines in place that stipulate its use.

Yes, there is the First Amendment, which protects free speech. What that actually means, however, seems to be up for debate. The only thing everyone warily agrees on is that you can't yell *"FIRE"* in a crowded theater.

That's about it.

Everything else, apparently, is up to us as individuals: our worldview, our beliefs, and our moral compass.

Is that enough?

Thoughts on Speaking
#thinkbeforeyouspeak

*Is it truthful?
*Is it necessary?
*Is it kind?
*Does it improve
 on the silence?

A compilation of guidelines on thoughtful speaking
– BUDDHA / BERNARD MELTZER

The power of language lies in its ability to deliver nuance, context, and specificity.

These are qualities that are hard to come by in modern life. We hurry from content to event, from work to workout, from soundbite to soundbite. We copy and paste, and we speak in sweeping generalizations.

And more often than not, we ignore the nuance, the specifics, the context—the fine print.

WELCOME TO THE ATTENTION ECONOMY

On the surface, it seems evident that our current lifestyles, with access to every thing at every turn of every action—yet little time to really absorb any of it—have opened the door for social media to shred substance into tiny hits of visual dopamine.

Our lifestyles demand more of our time and attention, accelerating an already vicious cycle.

The limit of language is tied to our capacity to <u>listen</u>.

Communication is a two-way street. It requires a sender and at least one receiver.

And that receiver, ideally, does more than just record data. Information needs to be decoded, interpreted. Meaning must be attached. This involves education and experience, data crunching, and mental presence.

With social media, we have built extraordinary tools for shouting. We don't, however, have equivalent tools for listening.

Yet, it would serve us well to occasionally pause the yapping and start paying attention.

*Because if we don't listen,
language loses its power.*

Are we regressing from substance to soundbite?

In private, substance seems to be hanging on. In the public square, on the other hand, soundbites have a much greater chance of gaining traction.

Substance has been submerged.

Surprising? Not really. Brands, by their necessity to be recalled, tend to flatten complexity. This gives them the stealth to reach into our private lives, homes, bedrooms, drawers, and, now, pockets, wrestling for our attention like never before.

How much attention can we really
give each interruption?

Nuanced policy discussions [. . .] will almost certainly get simplified into 'meaningless slogans' in order to travel farther online, and politicians will continue to stake out more extreme positions and commandeer news cycles."

– CHARLIE WARZEL
On Michael Goldhaber / The New York Times

Substance

Will this species tweet itself to death?

We are perpetually in search of shortcuts.

Human beings go through life as a kind of conduit, or connector, between our internal lives and the external world we live in.

We are forced to process an external reality that is ever-increasing in complexity. At the same time, our brains are perpetually crunching the data of our internal worlds.

All day. Every day.

So we can't really blame our brains for being on the prowl for shortcuts wherever possible. We commonly skip over words in a text and make snap judgements about people, circumstances, and things.

And are drawn to symbols like moths to a flame.

POST
SYMBOL
BITES!
TWEET™
SCREAM
SOUND
BITES
SOUNDBITES!
SYMBOL
SOUNDBITES
POST™
SYMBOL
SOUNDBITE
SYMBOL
TWEE
My Mental Carousel
PLAY

When language falls short, <u>symbols</u> step in.

The symbol is the ultimate visual soundbite. It is the simplest possible way to represent ideas, products, beliefs, political views, events, and religions.

The power of symbols lies not only in their mythically captivating powers but in their ability to send signals across cultures and language.

It is therefore not surprising that, as the world has grown more interconnected through commerce at ever-increasing speeds, symbols have amassed more and more power.

This is the point at which we come full circle.

*Most other, more complex symbols
are derived from these basic shapes.*

Triangle 🔍

A triangle is used to represent *revelation, harmony, creativity,* and *enlightenment*. Its three corners are often used to symbolize *various trinities:* mind-body-spirit, father-son-Holy Ghost, mother-father-child, past-present-future.

Circle 🔍

The circle is often used to represent the notions of *totality, wholeness,* and *original perfection.* Because there is no beginning or end, it can symbolize the infinite nature of energy or the inclusivity of the universe.

Square 🔍

The square represents *structure, logic,* and *order.* Its four sides are also related to the four physical elements in our universe: earth, air, water, and fire.

Symbols have become cultural markers, iconography steeped with meaning for people to rally around or find inspiration in.

When we think of ancient Egypt, familiar images promptly spring to mind: the eye of Horus, serpents, falcons, bare-chested gods, jackal-headed guardians, and vulture-winged goddesses.

When we think of the Maya and Aztecs or the Romans and Greeks of antiquity, we recall their distinct garb, their monuments, their symbolic motifs, or we may recall their enduring myths—all reflections of a particular cultural essence that, when taken together, uniquely defines and represents the culture and time period.

SYMBOLS STAND FOR SOMETHING

An object. An idea. A product. A service. A belief system. A way of navigating the world we live in.

The shape of a symbol is <u>assigned</u>. Its meaning is usually <u>acquired</u>.

It is that meaning—that emotional substance at the heart of symbols—that gives them their superhuman powers. They offer momentary reprieve from our brains—an off button to our perpetual junk generator—and a fleeting connection to something deeper within us and larger outside of us.

It is the goal of the symbol makers to harness that emotional power.

Symbols connect us.

**Symbols
drive
us
apart.**

Are these symbols or logos? Icons?

Symbols help us navigate everyday life.

Symbols are sometimes literal and sometimes not.
At times they need decoding; other times they don't.

Either way, they stand in for our hopes and dreams.
Occasionally, they stand in for our darkest fears.

They offer us a lifeline or an anchor.

Sometimes, they even set us free.

But what if we take symbols out of context?

What if we take an ancient symbol into modern times and turn it into a logo?

What happens when our world is full of iconography that is no longer attached to creation myths, cultural history, and religious ideas?

What happens when symbols are running amuck, divorced from any commonly understood meaning?

What happens when a culture's most potent symbols are aligned with profit-driven corporate entities and the products they want us to buy?

Does it change us?

For millennia, symbols have transported us.
They have guided us.
They have illuminated our paths.

Symbols have put the fear of god in us.
Literally.

Symbols often elicit an immediate emotional reaction.

Much like the power button on a TV set, symbols have the ability to activate our emotional reservoirs. They allow us to recall vast libraries of information, stories, and experiences.

Because of that power, they have been used and abused, refurbished and repurposed.

The original swastika, derived from the Sanskrit "svastika," was believed to be a positive symbol, encouraging of life. Until it wasn't.

We use symbols to oppress the others.

For as long as stories and symbols have existed, we have divided ourselves around them. We are divided over the right way to pray, what to wear, and who we are allowed to love.

When large groups of people rally around the fictional narratives tied to symbols, it can lead to an inflated sense of self and a feeling of superiority over others who rely on a different story about their place in the world. These tales have been used to conquer lands and extinguish or indoctrinate people of different beliefs.

We have raped and murdered. Annexed and pillaged. Conquered and converted. We have done so with language, with symbols of faith, governance, and commerce.

At the heart of these movements, deep in the epicenter of hate, are the graphic symbols that become part of people's identities.

We have used stories to create "the others" and forced symbols upon them to label them as such.

We use symbols to express ourselves.

However, when we mark ourselves, symbols take on an entirely different meaning.

They become symbols of freedom.
Symbols of non-conformity. Or lack thereof.

They become symbols of belonging.

The terms *symbol, mark, icon,* and *logo* are often used interchangeably. And in most cases, that works just fine.

Logos like Coca-Cola® are often referred to as logotypes or wordmarks.

Symbol

A symbol is a mark, sign, or word that is broadly understood to represent an *idea*, an *object*, or a *relationship*.

Symbols can take different forms: words, sounds, gestures, or images.

Icon

An icon is a *pictorial representation* of what it stands for. It resembles more closely the object depicted.

Logo

A logo is a *graphic mark*, *symbol*, or *stylized word* that identifies a company, product, organization, or brand. It can be abstract or figurative.

The word *logo* is more often used in a commercial context.

It is possible for a universal symbol to be turned into a logo for commercial purposes. Usually, this means it gets altered or combined with other visual elements.

Universal symbol for love.

® Registered for commercial use.

Symbol of Neptune, Greek god.

Symbol of Aphrodite, Greek goddess.

Symbols—or logos—usually need to be infused with meaning.

That meaning is usually acquired through either _time_ or _money_. Ancient symbols, for example, have had decades, centuries, even millennia to become what they stand for today, while newly minted marks are often introduced to the world through expensive marketing campaigns.

Their ultimate effect is achieved through design, the product itself, its usefulness, and the emotional resonance of the product for the consumer.

> "It is foolhardy to believe that a logo will do its job immediately, before an audience has been properly conditioned."
>
> **– PAUL RAND**

Logos transcend language.

They are shorthand—
CliffsNotes®—to the world
of commerce, politics, and
spirituality.

And most often, they fail
to deliver ~~nuance, context,~~
and ~~specificity.~~

Those failures can curb a logo's reach and emotional appeal. Nevertheless, its powers can often feel almost limitless because its meaning is open to interpretation.

It can mean different things to different people.

An Apple logo might stand for the ingenuity and potential of the human race to some, while others may blame it for laying the foundation of the always-on culture we find ourselves in. Engineering cameras into every person's pocket has led to the exposure of police brutality on one hand, but also to the growing pressures of having to perform our lives for a social media audience on the other.

And yes, all of these things can be true at the same time.

We might be fueled by brands, but we are <u>linked</u> through logos.

BLM marches in London.
The Happiest Place On Earth™ in China.
Doctors Without Borders.
Pro-democracy protests in Russia.
Amazon in … the Amazon?

This is the world of global marketing campaigns and supply chains.

Across borders, cultures, and language, we are inevitably connected through the symbols that represent products, movements, and ideas.

Sometimes, language helps define logos.

Frequently, language accompanies logos in the form of a tagline. This is often the case when a new brand is first introduced in order to give it more context.

For more established brands, taglines often support marketing campaigns, which tend to change more frequently than the brand itself. Campaign language gives the brand the flexibility to evolve from season to season, product to product, click to click.

Much like a compass, it guides a brand in a specific direction for a specific journey.

JUST LIKE IT.

Why don't you?

Logo ≠ Brand

Brands transcend logos.
They are part art and part science.

A great brand is much like a chemical compound: it is difficult to separate out the different components because they perform in perfect harmony of design, message, and product.

Brands are built around their visual identity—which the logo is part of—but also their voice, their behavior, and their rituals, all of which affect the experience an audience, customer, or follower has with the brand.

We find ourselves relying on an ever-increasing compilation of brands for everything from ordering groceries to sending valentines.

Brands that curate. Brands that govern. Brands that imagine. Brands that sell. Brands that inform. Brands that organize. Brands that manufacture. Brands that <u>are humans.</u>

Social media has given rise to ordinary humans as brands. Many of us are obsessively curating highlight reels of our lives.

We shape our identities on these platforms with purpose. Even people who consciously decide not to participate in the contest of personal popularity send a signal through their refusal to do so.

The choices we make in private define our public personas. So do the decisions of which brands we associate ourselves with.

And no, most of us do not have personal logos. We do, however, apply tools of branding to shape our public perception.

"We are all just actors trying to control and manage our public image, we act based on how others might see us."

– ERVING GOFFMAN

"The only way to make sense out of change is to plunge into it, move with it, and join the dance."

– Alan Wilson Watts

ANTLERS. ANGELS. ABSOLUT (Vodka!): who's ready for the holidays??

We have forever been linked through <u>love.</u>

Most of us just want to fit in. We crave belonging to something bigger than ourselves. We want to feel needed, connected. We want to be seen for who we are and accepted for who we want to be.

We use the tools of branding not purposely to pursue some sort of larger agenda. We use them because we want to look good, feel good.

We post pictures of our kids because we're proud of them. We publish anniversary wishes to our spouses because we love them. And we want the world to know it—even though we could just as easily whisper it across the breakfast table.

How, then, did life turn into something that needs to be performed, not lived?

69 Comments

Everything branding is expanding. Including what it is to be a brand.

The aperture of what is considered a brand is opening.

In my view, it incorporates institutions or individuals who participate in the public sphere with the goal of selling their product or promoting their opinion in exchange for some sort of currency or capital.

In many ways, the application of the branding process has been turned upside down; once adopted to mark our belongings, we now more often use its tools to fit in, somewhere, somehow. To belong to something.

Or to create communities that large groups of people want to belong to.

What is it that we want?

Branding captures the spiritual essence of a thing and gives it physical shape.

It transports ideas into the minds of human beings.

It assigns _value and virtue_ to objects and actions and sends a memorable signal into the universe.

It codifies _patterns and practices_ that become the internal foundation of a brand.

It connects physical things with the mental picture of what they stand for and what they mean to our lives.

It connects our internal and external worlds.

It links symbolism and experience.

It bridges fantasy and reality.

It creates a shorthand for compartmentalizing the increasing complexities of life.

Branding 🔍

Branding is the purposeful shaping of public perception.

The process of branding can be applied to almost anything; most often, this is a product, a place, or a person.

Brand 🔍

A brand is the way a corporation (or individual) *presents its product or service* in the market-place to make it recognizable to potential buyers.

The product can be an object, a person, a service, an opinion, or a worldview.

Brand vs. Corporation 🔍

The most straightforward way to think of a corporation (or company, which is smaller) is as the *sum of the people* that work for it.

We are currently linked through likes.

Social media connects us in a way we've never been connected before. A human web of extraordinary potential, it has, however, regressed into a monstrous machine for mining likes. From friends. From strangers. From people who behave like brands and brands that behave like people.

Yes, people can be brands. But, of course, they're not born that way. At some point in life, we all become conscious of how our appearance, our behavior, and our communication affect our surroundings.

And when we start to consciously shape appearance, messaging, and behavior, we employ tools of branding.

But we're not a brand. Yet.

Is that line crossed when our identity is exchanged for something of value?

Like this?

And we are, unfortunately, linked through lies.

While dubious ideas and dangerous movements have found willing followers throughout history, social media has enabled this venom to spread with unprecedented velocity and viciousness.

Like any organization, these movements are defined by the symbols and stories people rally around.

But make no mistake. These are brands, willfully and purposely crafted around ideas of hate. And lies.

And yes, social media companies are making profits from the distribution of hate.

The white supremacist version of the Celtic Cross, which consists of a square cross interlocking with or surrounded by a circle, is one of the most important and commonly used white supremacist symbols.

– ANTI-DEFAMATION LEAGUE

QAnon is a far-right conspiracy theory alleging that a cabal of Satan-worshipping cannibalistic pedophiles is running a global child sex-trafficking ring and plotting against U.S. President Trump.

– WIKIPEDIA

The "Sonnenrad" or sunwheel is one of a number of ancient European symbols appropriated by the Nazis in their attempt to invent an idealized "Aryan/Norse" heritage.

– ANTI-DEFAMATION LEAGUE

The brand hardens and shelters the lie.

From the LOST CAUSE of the Confederacy to the most recent BIG LIE of election fraud, brands have been built around lies so large they defy rational thought.

The brand—just like the scar tissue that restores the skin after contact with a sizzling iron—solidifies that false narrative. It often rewrites history, hardening the glaze in the kiln of conspiracy and making the lie strong enough to mobilize the masses.

"It (the lie) must be protected, reinforced, practiced in rituals and infused with symbols."

– DAVID W. BLIGHT / The New York Times

Tips on Controlling the Masses!
#neveroutofstyle

⋯

*"The great masses of people will more easily fall
victim to a big lie than a small one."*

*"If you tell a big enough lie and tell it frequently
enough, it will be believed."*

*"Make the lie big, make it simple, keep saying it,
and eventually they will believe it."*

*"By the skillful and sustained use of propaganda,
one can make a people see even heaven as hell
or an extremely wretched life as paradise."*

Quotes from MEIN KAMPF
– ADOLF HITLER

Brands are a *MEDIUM FOR THE <u>MASSES</u>.*

Because the *MASSES CRAVE A <u>MESSAGE</u>.*

"We are dominated by the relatively small number of persons who understand the mental processes and social patterns of the masses. It is they who pull the wires which control the public mind."

– EDWARD BERNAYS

Mass media, however—defined for decades by three major television networks—has been replaced by a fractured landscape littered with content hubs that seem to be splintering further and further away from a sense of shared reality.

The right watches FOX.
The left watches MSNBC.

Microbrands like blogs, newsletters, and a plethora of digital "news" brands fill out that scene, making it easy to find content that caters to our values, musical tastes, and political views.

This leaves us connected to people who think like us, yet isolated from the others.

"We're bowling alone or at least only with people who resemble us, and agree with us, in nearly every conceivable way."

– SUBDIVIDED WE FALL by **SCOTT STOSSEL** / The New York Times

Brands are human constructs.

They are rooted in the stories we tell each other in order to fulfill the fundamental need to belong that simmers at the core of human existence.

Religion, race, money, the stock market:
All of these are human constructs.

Much like the principle of Schrödinger's cat, brands are suspended in a contradictory state of opposition: They exist, but if we weren't there to observe them, or let them stir our emotions, they would simply vanish into thin air.

Of course, this could be said for any human creation, or the falling tree in the forest. It is, however, especially relevant for brands because they are purposely shaped to shape perception.

They are, therefore, both real and imaginary. They elicit real emotions by tapping into our imaginations.

Brands are both essentially meaningless and existentially meaningful.

Objectively, there is not much difference between these two approaches to delivering information.

U.S. DEPARTMENT OF
HOMELAND SECURITY

*Yet, who would you rather have
knocking on your door?*

It is the identity of the agencies we interact with that shapes the narrative of our governments.

Many of the departments that make up the bureaucratic apparatus of a government have a tendency to present themselves in a rather menacing manner.

These brands are often militarized.

Weapons of war—machinery of offense and defense—are used to symbolize . . . what exactly? A nation that will defend itself? From whom? A nation that will attack its neighbors? Its citizens? The others?

And yes, we (still) live in a militarized world.

Brands are markers in our physical and digital worlds.

Imagine a shopping mall without a single store sign. You would have to enter every store to find out what product each of them sells and whether it is the one you came for.

It is easy to see how brands are both informational and emotional guides in our daily lives.

COME

AND

HERE

LOVE

ME

We live in a brand-space construct.

PERCEPTION

ATTENTION

And, much like black holes distort physical space around them, this branded universe we inhabit bends our attention to its will. And it has our perceptions—of ourselves, the world, of others—wrapped around its gravitational forces.

It makes us see and feel things
that may or may not be real.

Commerce, religion, and politics all employ tools of branding to extend invitations for people to join their causes or buy their products.

At their best, these are carefully crafted and cultivated symbols of belonging.

The tangible joy of your morning coffee shop routine.

The flag of safe harbor after a long journey at sea.

The cross against the sky welcoming a congregation of the like-minded.

These are symbols of optimism and hope.

On the other side, these same tools of branding have been employed throughout history to oppress people of different skin color, different belief, different sexual orientation—the others.

To sow discord. Attack enemies, real or perceived.

They have been used by dictators, autocrats, kings, and ruling elites to pit groups of people against one another in order to consolidate their grip on power.

These are symbols of division and hate.

Unfortunately, the power to unify on one hand also has the potential to divide on the other.

Branding creates allies and adversaries.

For better or worse, brands create order in the universe.

They organize people, products, and politics around different value systems.

It is by revisiting these systems that we can begin to chart a path toward a new future.

Have our priorities fallen out of balance? Have they ever really been in balance? What are the roads through this treacherous world that lies before us? Is this the only way forward? To let the world fall to pieces while the vultures peck over its remains and we passively amuse ourselves to death?

Not if we wake up.

Not if we take a step back and look at the bigger picture.

Act 3.

A New World Brand

Go Humans!!!

We are fortunate to be cast for a tiny part in a giant cosmic play.

Because the odds of getting this role—human life—are very slim. That's just science.

THE GREAT

STORY

Their survival depends on one thing only:

CAN THEY GET ALONG?

Starring humans.
And a tiny planet drifting in a giant universe.

HMNKND
PRODUCTIONS

ESBIANS. IRANIANS. PANSEXUALS
WS. GERMANS. GERMOPHOBES.
VES. CANADIANS. HOMOSEXUAL
TINOS. MULATTOS. BLACKS. WH
RS. DESIGNERS. ZOOPHOBIANS. E
REAMERS. CLERKS. PROGRAMME
EMOCRATS. REPUBLICANS. CORF
OUNTAIN CLIMBERS. MONOSEXU
NGE WATCHERS. ACTIVISTS. PAC
ARMERS. ELITES. ESSENTIAL WOR
EXUALS. AUTOSEXUALS. RISK TAK
ROCRASTINATORS. PERUVIANS. F
TS. GLOBALISTS. PACIFISTS. EXT
IALISTS. SOCIALITES. CAPITALIST
EALISTS. FUTURISTS. IMPRESSION
ARIANS. CATHOLICS. PROTESTAN
ATIVES. DOUBTERS. BELIEVERS. B
ANITES. URBANITES. OPTIMISTS. S
TAS. BARISTAS. PESSIMISTS. FOO
OLITICIANS. PROLETARIAT. HINDU

EXUALS. AMERICANS. TEACHERS.
ESTINIANS. LIBERALS. CONSERVA
ONDURANS. PATIENTS. DOCTORS
. BUSSERS. PATRONS. NURSES. M
HERS. SISTERS. PSYCHOLOGISTS
REALISTS. NATURALISTS. NUDIST:
ATIONS. TRUMPERS. THRILL SEEK
. METROSEXUALS. COUCH SURFE
TS. POLICE OFFICERS. INFLUENCI
S. SEX WORKE   EX SEEKERS.
. FAKERS. FINI   . SELF-START
ICIANS. POLYSEXUALS. EXHIBITIC
ERTS. INTROVERTS. PET LOVERS.
UMANISTS. IMPORTERS. EXPORTE
. ACTIVISTS. ANARCHISTS. LIBER
UDDHISTS. IDEALISTS. IMMIGRAI
IANS. BOTOXERS. BISEXUALS. SUI
TUALISTS. INDUSTRIALISTS. FASH
. NUDIES. PUNKS. COUCH POTATC
PPIES. HIPSTERS. BOLIVIANS. BRC

All of us.

And yes, this includes the others, because the others are real. They are more than labels. They have faces and fears.

They might have taken different paths to get to here and now. They might have created different myths. Different heroes and different villains. They might use different sounds and symbols. They might have written different origin stories.

But they have a part in the same play, the one written for all of us by an invisible hand.

Science. Almighty. God. Allah. Buddha. Christ.

These are pseudonyms for the same author of the same great story. The one we all belong to.

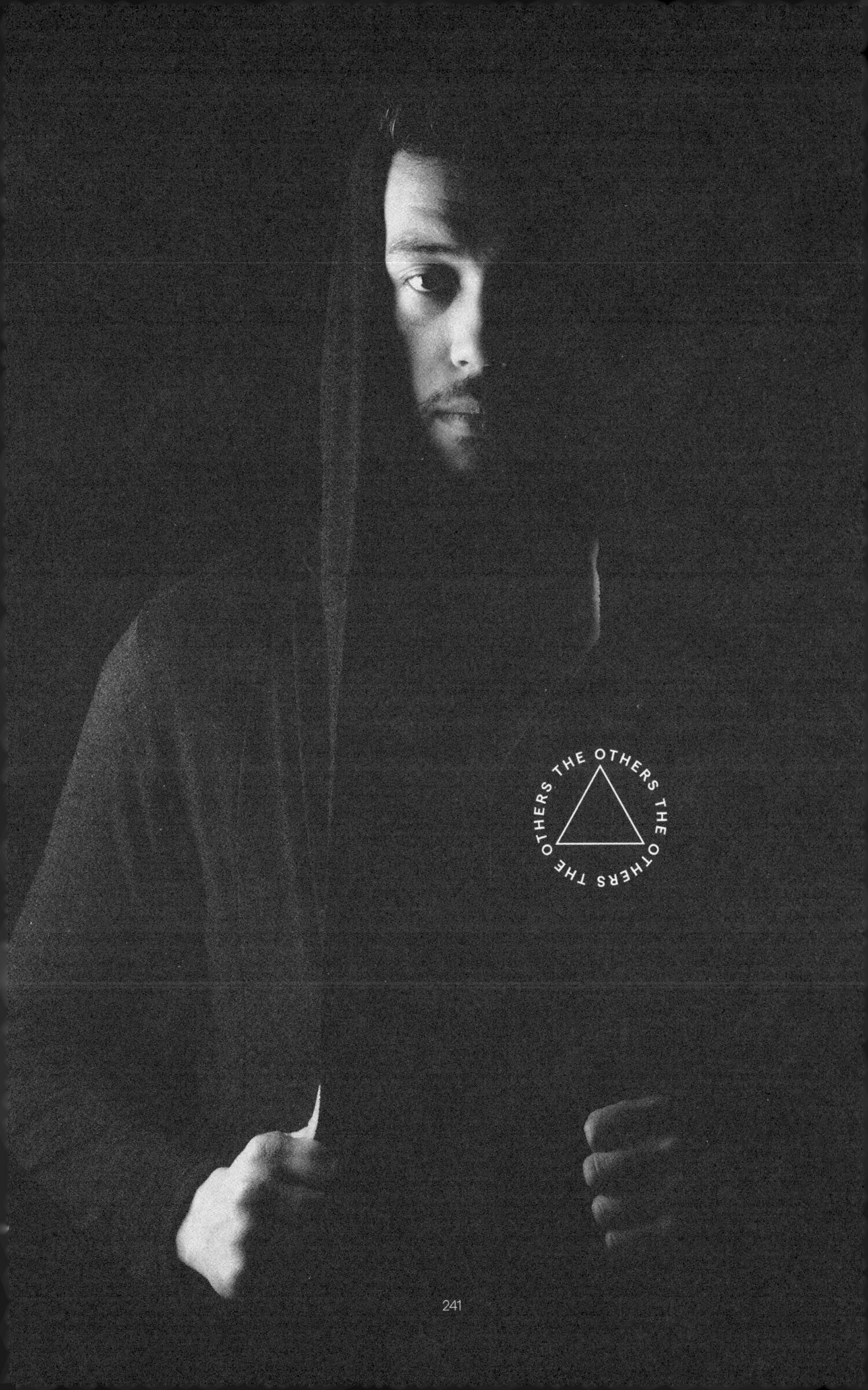
THE OTHERS THE OTHERS THE OTHERS

The story of us is the greatest story ever told.

It recounts improbable origins. Stories of survival, adaptation, human collaboration, and perseverance.

It narrates our struggle. War. Loss. Perseverance, yet again. And the rebuilding to even greater heights.

This story depicts the most remarkable achievements accomplished by people exercising their own free will. But, in reality, this is often attained at the expense of other people. Through forced labor and slavery. At the peril of the planet through industrial production and modern means of transportation. At the expense of each other through the betrayal and corruption of the very social structures we built.

This story is as old as time.

This Is Not A Drill

▼

And yes, we are dangerously close to squandering our cosmic gift of living on the one speck in the known universe capable of sustaining life.

So now what?

We need to accept our story. The others. And ourselves.

Sure, let's appreciate our achievements. But let's also accept our flawed histories, our false narratives, our destructive nature, and our perpetual struggles to be better.

We need to reframe the stories that divide us into stories that unite us. *Not in a marketing or political bullshit kind of way. Or a Zen-Kumbaya kind of way.*

In an existential, "if we don't, there won't be a story to tell" kind of way.

"I don't think you can truly change for the better in a lasting, meaningful way unless it is driven by self-acceptance."

– BRENÉ BROWN

An update is available for your system.
This update requires consideration of the following:

- ☑ Accepting responsibility for our wrongs of the past

- ☑ Accepting truths that do not fit into our worldview

- ☑ Giving up things that weren't ours in the first place

- ☑ Prioritizing purpose over profit

- ☑ Being open to change in good faith

Use of this update is subject to self-acceptance.

What if we don't?

*What happens when we're promised land but
never receive it?*

*What happens if we're told fracking is safe, but
the ground starts to shake beneath our feet?*

*What happens when you don't know anymore if a
news story is true?*

*What happens if you're told your insurance covers
your medical condition but you find out it doesn't?*

*What happens when you can't be sure what
"organic" means?*

*What happens if your drinking water is deemed
safe, but you get poisoned with every sip?*

*What happens when an entire political party
declares war on the truth?*

*What happens when you're fed stories of equality
but are arrested for the color of your skin?*

*What happens if large parts of a population live
in opposing media ecosystems?*

That's more than many of us can handle. It leads to
chaos, confusion, and *contempt*. And what's pushing
us over the edge are brands with questionable morals,
corrupt intent, or good old-fashioned greed.

Chaos:
Theory or Culture?

Disinformation has always been part of the political and corporate playbook. However, algorithms, feedback loops, and political polarization have dusted off that book and put it on the main display next to the ChapStick® and gummy bears.

This is complex stuff, and only a few people in the world seem to truly comprehend the scientific underpinnings of the madness we've let ourselves be swallowed up in.

Chaos theory? Or chaos culture?

If the <u>medium is the message</u> and the medium is a giant tangled ball of fiber-optic cables, doesn't that make the message, well, a giant tangled mess of messaging?

Amidst the chaos, however, human beings are—and always have been—capable of extraordinary feats.

We built the Large Hadron Collider. A global network for commercial air travel. The International Space Station. Shared ventures shouldered through collaboration across continents, cultures, space, and time.

Like other globally significant public projects, our modern information delivery systems have been decades in the making.

We have connected digital devices by laying cables into every last corner of the earth, over mountains and under oceans. We have built data centers and imagined digital clouds out of thin air.

These are marvels of
engineering and technology.

And into this essentially egalitarian and frictionless superstructure, we dropped a powerful new element: social media.

Like a sluggish chemical reaction, this great experiment—branded and marketed as the ultimate tool of techno-utopian democracy—started off quietly: personal blogs gave enthusiastic individuals a platform to express themselves.

Gradually, established and emerging actors—good, greedy, and bad—poured into this petri dish, igniting an explosive chain reaction, turning the experiment into the internet we know today: information traveling at near the speed of light, with few guardrails or gate-keepers, fact crashing into fiction, splintering into an indecipherable universe of digital dust.

Turning brands into bullets in the barrel of the internet.

And things are about to get worse.

For decades, the technology to create digital humans and figures with lifelike features was only available to big-budget feature filmmakers. But the rapid rise of GPU processing power and advances in machine learning are already filtering selfies beyond recognition across social media, and increasingly, fully digital "people" are populating our virtual worlds.

From fake human service reps to fake human dating bots to friends with fake faces, how will we see ourselves and relate to each other when we aren't sure who is a real flesh-and-blood human . . . and who is a digital mirage?

How will we be able to trust anything we see and hear?

Consider every daily action or interaction that calls for an almost superhuman level of trust in other humans. Trust in the fact that they have done their job to keep you or your loved ones safe, or provided true and accurate information.

Reading an article.
Dropping off your toddler at preschool.
Casting your vote.
Getting on an airplane. Into a car. Onto the subway.
Shopping for groceries.
Getting a vaccine.

Almost everything in our daily lives requires a lengthy global supply chain of trust, with each step calling for lawful and ethical conduct by people responsible for completing that step.

And yes, that's a lot of trust.

Somehow, we have to find a way to regain that trust in each other, in our actions and the symbols we share.

Without trust in the meaning of those symbols and the conduct they lead to, we could not have coordinated our hunt for food, warned other members of our tribe of imminent danger, or built roads for the newly invented wheel.

Without agreement on the meaning of language, we couldn't have printed the Gutenberg Bible, written the Declaration of Independence, or penned letters of eternal love.

And we wouldn't be bonding over Spider-Man.

My dearest Angelica,
What happens to us
without trust?

Consider this:

An automotive company attempts to increase sales. The marketing team develops a campaign promoting upgrades to an old technology and reducing vehicle emissions by an unfathomable amount, therefore making its products better for the environment than its competition.

The company's scientists, however, fail to make the technology live up to its claims. In order to meet the sales targets, the engineers—without doubt some of the best and brightest in the industry—invent a device to deceive the emission tests, continuing to pollute the environment in drastic excess of its competition.

This is what happens when marketing drives the product.

Former Volkswagen CEO charged with fraud in Germany

German prosecutors have indicted former Volkswagen CEO Martin Winterkorn and four others on charges of fraud and unfair competition

– DAVID McHUGH / AP Business Writer

The New York Times

©2017 The New York Times

$6.00

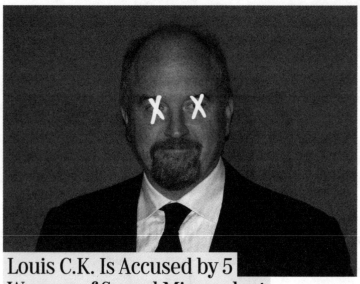

Louis C.K. Is Accused by 5
Women of Sexual Misconduct

Consider this:

A comedian breaks into the mainstream by leaning into his average physical appearance, out-of-shape "dad body," and resulting sexual misadventures.

He is authentic.
He is relatable.
He is everywhere.

Yet the **#METOO** movement doesn't come to a halt at the doorsteps of comedy clubs and television specials. His show is canceled, he swiftly disappears from our television screens, and an adoring audience is left with not just the loss of their refuge in humor but an emotional connection and trust that has been broken.

Consider this:

"70 percent of people outside the United States have no confidence in President Trump to do the right thing in world affairs. This negative perception has had reper-cussions for America's international image, with views toward the United States at historic lows in many coun-tries—well below the overwhelmingly positive views during the Obama presidency."

– ALEXANDER AGADJANIAN & YUSAKU HORIUCHI / The Washington Post

Let's make the argument that the core of USA™—the brand—doesn't change very often.

The Constitution, flaws and all, remains at the center of this grand experiment we call democracy.

What changes every four or eight years are the priorities and policies, the actions and reactions of the people elected to run this gigantic machine.

And the institutional dishonesty and blatant corruption we have seen over the last few years has led to a steep decline in trustworthiness, which, in turn, has led to the plummeting perception of the greatest brand in history across the globe.

It takes a lot to get that back.

At their core, these are stories of <u>trust</u>. And <u>truth</u>.

Stories of character, or the lack thereof. These are stories of beliefs and make-believe.

They are, therefore, stories of branding.

Consider the brand promise* of the finest food. The fastest internet. The most relaxing vacation. The best education. The lowest emissions. The most dramatic entertainment.

If any of those promises are not your lived experience with any given brand, your trust in that brand is broken.

Instantly. Possibly irrevocably.

Twitter tantrums.
Yelp! yelps.
Facebook freakouts.

---

*Welcome to another gray zone! Is it the <u>brand</u> that makes these claims, or is it <u>marketing</u> that tries to sell you on the benefits of the brand?

"If the truth doesn't matter, we're lost."

– ADAM SCHIFF / Representative (CA 28th District)

Brands are built on trust. And trust can only be built on a foundation of truth.

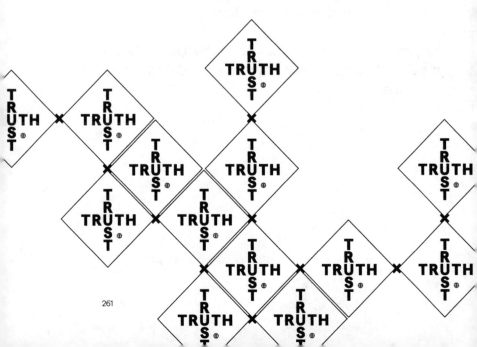

Branding is a tool to get to the truth.⊤

At its core, the process of branding is amoral. The art and science of distilling a thing* down to its essence is neither inherently good nor fundamentally bad. It all depends on what we use it for.

Junk in. Junk out.

We have built magnificent machines.

Of commerce, communication, transport.
Of citizenry. And yes, of branding.

Yet, machines require maintenance. Upgrades. New hardware and operating systems. Updated filters for junk and malware.

*Traditionally a product, service, place, or person.

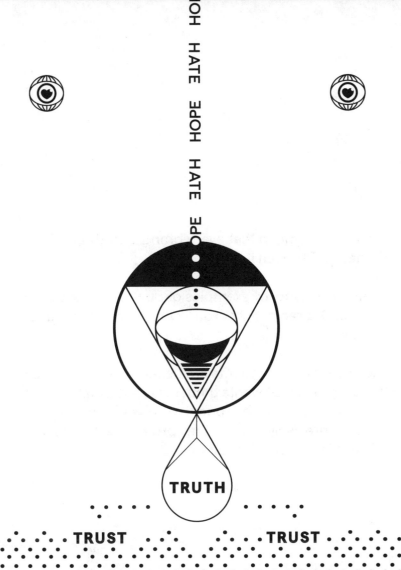

HOPE HATE HOPE HATE HOPE

TRUTH

TRUST TRUST

Belonging!

This doesn't mean that every brand is truthful in its behavior. Far from it.

There are plenty of examples of powerful brands built on lies. Or brands built around products intended to do harm.

However, those products are usually geared toward a target group that wants them for exactly <u>that</u> purpose. One could therefore argue that those brands are truthful precisely to what they promise: lies, hate, fear, or, worse, the destruction of life.

CNBC

Alex Jones' 5 most disturbing and ridiculous conspiracy theories

– TUCKER HIGGINS

1. *The government has "weather weapons"*

2. *Chemicals in the water are turning frogs gay*

3. *Robert Mueller is a demon, and also a pedophile*

4. *The Sandy Hook shooting was staged*

5. *Hillary Clinton is running a child sex ring out of a pizza parlor*

Are these true beliefs?
Or lies pushed to further an agenda?

Branding should be a selfless act.

A great brand naturally flows out of the product or service. Graciously. Optimistically. With the singular focus of making it successful.

Yes, it needs shaping. Crafting. Articulating. But the underlying shape—the bones of whatever it is—are present from its inception.

And brand builders help it find the appropriate outfit, coach it on how to walk and how to talk, and set it free. So when it goes out into the world, its appearance matches its personality.

And no, selfless doesn't mean private.

Selfless? REALLY?

Isn't branding all about yourself?
Looking inward?
A transcendently selfish act?

Well, consider a brand part of society. And as it steps into the world, it is common courtesy to signal clearly what it stands for.

A brand doesn't live in isolation. Like the fish in water, which are dependent on an ecosystem around them, a brand on its own is a rather useless entity.

A mobile phone needs a cellular network, an electric infrastructure. It needs a marketplace for software, one for applications, and another one for accessories.

And each one of these ecosystems breaks down into smaller and smaller subsystems. Without any of which a cell phone is a useless brick of metal, plastic, and glass.

With a logo on the back.

If a brand lives by itself in the forest,
does anybody know it's a brand?

Evolutionarily, humans have always needed to strike a balance between focusing on the self and relying on the tribe. However, it seems that in these recent stages of our journey, we have become more and more obsessed with ourselves.

From customized meal-ordering services to targeted ads, we are putting the individual increasingly at the center of all human activity.

And sure, most of us like personalized meals as much as the next human. But there is an undercurrent of fear that this laser focus on ourselves and our own mortality has made us lose sight of the fact that we cannot thrive alone.

"Narcissism is the most shame-based of all the personality disorders. Narcissism is not about self-love at all. It's about grandiosity driven by high performance and self-hatred. I define it as the shame-based fear of being ordinary."

– BRENÉ BROWN

> ## "THE EGO IS BORN OUT OF FEAR AND ISOLATION."
>
> **– MARK EPSTEIN** / Psychotherapist

Is there a way to extinguish that fear?

It seems pretty simple:

We have to accept our insignificance. Which is <u>significant.</u>

If we were somehow able to change the lens through which we view our challenges and opportunities, recognize the big picture—THE GREAT STORY—we might find a way to comprehend how insignificant most of our conflicts are.

How much does it matter that the others believe a different story? Enough for disagreement? Sure.

But enough to spark hatred lasting generations? Draw permanent battle lines from which no side is willing to retreat? Enough to massacre for?

EDGE OF THE UNIVERSE
EDGE OF THE GALAXY
EDGE OF THE SOLAR SYSTEM

"With every step, every window that modern astrophysics has opened to our mind, the person who wants to feel like they're the center of everything ends up shrinking."

– NEIL DEGRASSE TYSON

CLIMATE CHANGE. MONEY IN POLIT
M. FOSSIL FUEL DEPENDENCY. INC
OLLUTION. ENDANGERED SPECIES
ON. WORLD HUNGER. CHILD MOI
ENCE. CLEAN WATER ACCESS. PO
WEAT SHOP L   TERRORISM.
L STUPIDITY   ATIONALISM
EPRODUCT   IONS. DISE
ONS. PRO   ITICAL V
OME IN   VIOLEN
MOTION   AL HEA
ON. CYBE   ELIGIOUS
ORPORATE   BILITIES. CO
RANCE. GENE   OLERANCE.
ACY. RISING A   RITARIANISM.
ATFISHING. WHI   COLLAR CRIM
ASS INCARCERATION. WAR ON D
UICIDE RATES. LINGUISTIC IMPERI
ATION. CATHOLIC SEX SCANDAL.
OLONIALISM. ELECTION FRAUD. C

It is only by
recognizing our
smallness that we can
begin to address the larger
issues that face the human race.

That's the story.

S. NET NEUTRALITY. POVERTY. RA(
ΛE INEQUALITY. GENDER INEQUA
EFORESTATION. OCEAN ACIDIFIC/
ITY. DISEASE. OBESITY. GUN VIO
CAL INSTABILITY. SEXUAL VIOLEN
RRUPTION. CRONYISM. WAR. GEN
NDEMICS. ACCESS TO HEALTHC
RANCHISEMENT. VOTING RESTRIC
ENCE. CAPITOL INSURRECTION. I
HATE CRIMES. SOCIAL ISOLATIO
GENERAL ANXIETY. DISINFORMA
LENCE. FOREVER WARS. NEPOTIS
-19. MASK WARS. POLITICAL INTC
HT WING EXTREMISM. ANTI-DEM
LATIONISM. INTERNET TROLLING
DCIAL INJUSTICE. OPIOID ADDICT
S. BULLYING. TEENAGE DEPRESS
SM. MORAL DECLINE. CHILD MOL
NOMIC OPPRESSION. CORPORA
SPIRACY THEORIES. WHITEWASH

At its core, branding is <u>storytelling</u>.

Whether it is a witty tweet, an outrageous outfit, or sustainable packaging that elevates your product, anything that shapes public perception adds a beat to the story.

A story about how we see the world.
A story about how we fit in.
A story about how we stand out.
A story that preys on our fears.
A story that paints a brighter future.
A story about our darker pasts.

Each one of us now has a pipeline to get our own narratives into the world—the tales of how we live, how we eat, and how we celebrate. What we buy, what we wear, and what we drive.

We are perpetually writing micro-chapters of THE GREAT STORY we inhabit. A story so complex it is easy to lose the underlying plot.

And yes, there is a hidden feature that defines the stories that drive our culture, the stories we lose ourselves in, and the stories that keep us up at night.

They are stories of **_conflict_**.

Conflict is what drives the narrative of feuding families.
Conflict is at the heart of crumbling kingdoms.
Conflict is what leads to backstabbing in boardrooms.

Conflict makes a good story. And yes, sadly, conflict is inevitably intertwined with the human experiment.

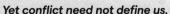
Yet conflict need not define us.

We need more stories of <u>compassion</u>, and fewer stories of conflict.

What's extraordinary about our story is that it is never complete. It is never finished. It is being written and rewritten every moment in every corner of the world.

For example, it is up to us to confine conflict to our books and films. Because for THE GREAT STORY to succeed, we need to course-correct away from conflict toward ***compassion*** and ***cooperation***.

We need to start shaping new stories for ourselves and future generations. And that narrative, in its most basic and simple form, might be this:

*Let's be kind to the planet we share
and the people we share it with.*

Sure, **we can tell each other that change is too hard.**

We've done it for many lifetimes.

It is the story of economic structures that are too complex and the influence of industries that are too powerful to change.

Yes, it is hard to stand up to the pressures of corporations with deep pockets. Yet shouldn't that lead us to question the role of money in politics, rather than the industry of progress?

And yes, we are challenging economic frameworks every day.

Sure, **we can convince each other that the gatekeepers are too mighty.**

Especially the newly installed ones.

The ones armed with algorithms and user data. The ones that have stockpiled more power in a shorter amount of time than any of the guards of previous generations. The ones that seem content to let the rest of us drown in hate, lies, misinformation, and conspiracy theories, as long as it bolsters their bottom line.

Yes, their lobbyists make up a formidable opponent on the battlefield of political mind-shaping.

Yet, shouldn't that lead us to question the industry of lobbying that works tirelessly to keep their clients safely stashed inside their pearly gates, out of reach of accountability and regulation—all while selling our data for profit?

We've toppled gatekeepers before.

Sure, we can proceed to massacre each other over our gods and titans.*

We can continue to stubbornly believe that the Second Amendment trumps all other human rights, including the right of our kids to go to school without fear of violence, and the right of our lawmakers to do their jobs without fear of deadly retribution.

Yet, our current condition has little to do with said Second Amendment. It seems more like a matter of private militias arming themselves for battle against the others than the right of citizens to bear arms for self-defense.

Is it any wonder that, under certain conditions, we turn this profusion of weaponry on each other?

That's how great empires fall—not through outside forces, but from within.

All of which are human inventions.

And sure, **we can maintain that laws are the only thing that should guide our economic behavior.**

However, just because you're all of a sudden allowed to drill on previously protected lands, does that mean that <u>you should?</u>

"Yes, our daily lives are undoubtedly contributing to climate change. But that's because the rich and powerful have constructed systems that make it nearly impossible to live lightly on the earth.

Our economic systems require most adults to work, and many of us must commute to work in or to cities intentionally designed to favor the automobile."

– EMMA MARRIS / The New York Times

New Drilling, Logging in Alaska's Protected
Areas Could Release as Much Pollution
as All the World's Cars Emit in a Year

– CENTER FOR AMERICAN PROGRESS

Or **we can wake up.**

We can acknowledge our shortcomings of the past.

We can admit that we know better now than we did when we set out on this journey of life, of humanity, and of societies.

We can admit that we have evolved and that we have come to understand that there is a better way.

We all need each other.
We are all vulnerable.
We all have the right to speak truth to power.

Let's rewrite our story.

If we can open ourselves to updating that narrative, we may find our minds open to changing our systems and structures.

Because our systems are antiquated. And many of our structures are relics of racism and oppression of the others. This may have gotten us to where we are today, but it won't get us where we need to go.

Because we have evolved as a species. And the stakes have changed.

"Capitalism is not immoral but amoral. It does what its users demand of it. It has given us a choice of food, travel and technology that kings could only dream of. It will invent whatever instruments governments and consumers want, and if not given limits, its inventiveness knows few bounds."

– **TIM MONTGOMERIE** / The Guardian

CAPITALISM

THE SYSTEM THAT
BROUGHT US PEACE

CAPITALISM

THE SYSTEM THAT
STRANGLED THE WORLD

The question is: WHICH story needs rewriting?

Critics of the system blame it for everything from the exploitation of the poor, to racial oppression, to the continuing destruction of our earthly habitat.

Supporters argue that trade among tribes is what has replaced war in many places. If we rely on somebody else to provide something we need, we are more likely to find diplomatic solutions to our disagreements. When countries need to trade with other countries, the conditions for conflict are drastically lowered.

Their belief in Adam Smith's stories remains resolute: self-interest produces for the public good.

Feels like both sides have a point?

Regardless of which story we subscribe to, most of us would probably agree with this:

Brands are much better than bombs!

And all sides might be persuaded that certain updates to the operating system would be in the interest of the entire species.

☀ **Checking for updates…**

OS El Capital

Version 2021.1

[System Report…] [System Update…]

If capitalism is the game, brands are the players.

They, too, are designed to be amoral. In theory.

Disregarding human "pollutants" like opinion, agenda, power, and greed, a brand is wrapped around a product that is exchanged in the marketplace for some kind of currency. And in order to sell as many units as possible, the product should come with an adequate price and quality, be truthful in its brand promises, and fulfill a need in the consumer.

If it does, it has a shot at being successful.

Those pollutants, however, are present at nearly every turn of capitalist transactions, sticking to us like grease from an oil spill.

Is it those pollutants that break our well-intentioned machines?

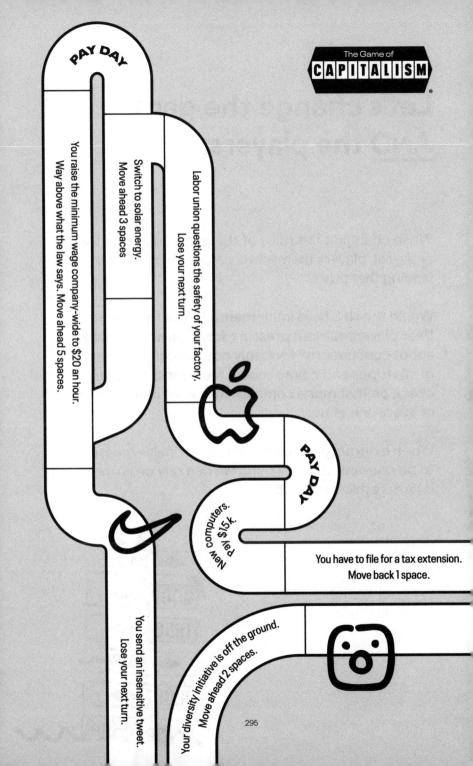

The Game of
CAPITALISM

PAY DAY

You raise the minimum wage company-wide to $20 an hour. Way above what the law says. Move ahead 5 spaces.

Switch to solar energy. Move ahead 3 spaces

Labor union questions the safety of your factory. Lose your next turn.

PAY DAY

New computers. Pay $15k.

You have to file for a tax extension. Move back 1 space.

You send an insensitive tweet. Lose your next turn.

Your diversity initiative is off the ground. Move ahead 2 spaces.

295

Let's change the game <u>AND</u> the players.

While changing the rules of the game has to be the end goal, players themselves can be instrumental in leading that push.

Would the NFL have implemented rules to protect their players without pressure from players worried about concussions? Probably not. Therefore, brands of all stripes and colors should feel emboldened to check on that moral compass that spins at the center of every one of us.

When external guidelines—and guardrails—cease to be relevant, the only thing we can rely on is our internal ethical makeup.

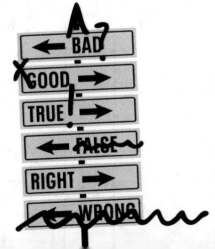

OS El Capital

Version 2021.1

System Report...   System Update...

An update is available for your system.
Before you update, please consider the following:

☐   Not paying our workers a living wage?

☐   Peddling misinformation?

☐   Trying to escape accountability?

☐   Ignoring environmental regulations?

☐   Supporting voter suppression?

☐   Not paying our fair share of taxes?

Use of this update is subject to general human decency.

Science* got us into this mess.

And by that I mean our blind trust in "man over nature."

I mean the ever more creative ways to suck energy out of the earth.

I mean the unmatched ability to engineer ourselves out of seemingly unsolvable problems.

I mean our intellectual capacity to fabricate stories of nationalism, religion, and rational justifications for trickle-down economics.

I mean the internet.

And I mean algorithms.

And sure, some other things, too.

Hu

"Life is too complicated for simple algorithms."

– NOAM CHOMSKY / The Ezra Klein Show

Science* will have to get us out of it.

And by science I don't mean flying cars, billionaire-financed rocket launches, the next-generation nuclear power reactor, or the colonization of Mars.

Sure, science may help us address the climate crisis.

It may help with exploring new energy sources.

It may help with the development of vaccines for the current and next global pandemic.

It may help filter hate from our digital bloodstreams.

But I also mean an adherence to basic facts, or some form of consensus-based truth.

Reason.
Fact.
Trust.

Truth.

*And sure, some other things, too.

Hu

●

Like, that the earth is round. And not created by an old white man. With a beard. In seven days.

And yes, it is fair to ask the question:

"What is truth?"

Is the truth that which we can observe and verify?

For example, we cannot personally verify the Big Bang. It's hard for us to personally observe climate change. Sure, the weather is getting noticeably weirder, and more extreme. But that's about it.

So why do I believe it to be an existential threat to our species? Because I believe in science? The scientists? Which one? All of them?

It's easy to see how the quest for truth can become a rabbit hole of galactic proportions.

"A lie gets halfway around the world before the truth has a chance to get its pants on."

– WINSTON CHURCHILL

Truth

Most scholars agree that truth is the state of being in accordance with reality. There are, however, disagreements about whether truth is absolute, or whether it can be relative to one's perspective.

Belief

Belief is the attitude an individual holds regarding anything they take to be true.

Justification

Justification is the reason someone holds a rationally admissible belief. Sources of justification might include personal perceptual experience, intellectual reasoning, and testimony by an authoritative figure.

However, a belief being justified does not guarantee that the belief is true.

 *The following are some of my personal truths, the ones I can justify with a good dose of rational thought.*

The truth is: **We need to wake our gatekeepers.**

They have been asleep at the pool. Soaking up the sun on the summit. Counting their loot. Looking the other way. Or worse even, actively amplifying the junk we put into our machines.

Let's ignore the fact that these challenges could not have been foreseen—a "move fast and break things" philosophy doesn't really lend itself to proper analysis and foresight—once the problem has come into focus, notably little has been done by any of the new media platforms to combat it.

If any other product resulted in "unforeseen" negative consequences, there likely would be government-mandated recall.

So to keep disinformation coming off the assembly line is irresponsible at best and malicious at worst.

"In order to have a functioning society, there has to be some understanding of objective truth. I worry we've lost that. And I would say right now we don't have a functioning society, partly because of Facebook and Twitter. They have no commitment to the objective truth, and no strategy on how to handle what they unleashed . . . Truth has to be defended, just like democracy."

– ROSE MARCARIO / CORNER OFFICE by **DAVID GELLES**
The New York Times

The truth is: **We need trust in <u>experts</u>, not influencers.**

While taste makers have always been a cultural force, social media has elevated them to a level of unproportional power over our lives.

The influencer's strength lies in their ability to attract followers across a plethora of media platforms. And the larger that herd, the bigger the clout of the taste maker. This potential to accumulate a seemingly unlimited amount of cultural currency is a unique and novel feature of our information age. In many ways, it is the logical result of the "egalitarian" society packaged and promoted by the internet pioneers.

However, the size of the crowd waiting to be influenced sometimes gives the influencer an inflated sense of their relevance.

That's not to say that an expert in beauty can't share their insight on parenting.

Sure. Please do that.
And thank you!

Yet, when "followers" take cues from their "leaders" on matters that affect the rest of us, things get complicated.

Vaccine advice from an NFL quarterback.
Personal attacks by a political pundit.
Election fraud claims from a reality TV star.

The triumph of the influencer is the logical end to the war on expertise that was launched decades ago. It is an uncivil war with casualties too many to count.

Yet, this war is far from over.

We need to restore experts to the status that has built the modern world we live in. The expertise that eradicated illnesses. The expertise that increased our mobility by the multiples. The expertise that built the tools we are now abusing to conduct a war on expertise in favor of influence.

We have to retreat from this self-inflicted conflict.
No matter how messy.

The truth is: **We need to cultivate curiosity.**

Curiosity is that strange human trait that got us out of the cave, across the globe, and onto the moon. The trait that has led to communication and collaboration.

It is why children ask: ***"Why?"***

And as we get older and life becomes more complicated, many of us forget to keep asking that question.

"Why?" requires work and critical thought. It requires the openness to learning answers that don't fit into our existing worldviews.

And sure, if we need to ask ***"Why?"*** every time we get a push notification on our phones, it will mercilessly take over our lives.

But it's also the most significant tool in combatting disinformation. And decoding the true intention of certain brands.

Curiosity might help us better understand the others.

Their intentions.
Their feelings and fears.

Curiosity might help us understand ourselves.

Our intentions.
Our feelings and fears.

Certain meditation techniques encourage us to approach our emotions with curiosity. We cannot control when and how those emotions arise within us, but we can control how we react to them.

The ancient principle of Occam's razor invites us to—when presented with competing hypotheses about the same problem—select the one that requires the fewest possible assumptions.

This might benefit us in our external *and* internal lives.

The truth is: **We need to save the truth seekers.**

Journalism, like many other disciplines, is not immune to the brand industrial complex.

Branded content, corporate "studies," and brand journalism are all vehicles for brands with means to sell their products and push their agendas. Disguised as serious journalism, these techniques can often turn into a Trojan horse of mass mind-shaping.

Sometimes transparent, more often opaque, they bet on big words to catch our attention, yet rely on fine print to veil their true personas.

One cable news network says the sky is up, while the other one says the sky is down. This shapes the reality of respective audiences in opposing ways and makes living in a shared world extremely difficult.

Journalism

Journalism is the creation and distribution of reports describing current events. It is based on facts, supported by evidence.

Journalism is <u>factual</u>.

It may be distributed through different types of media outlets: print, podcasts, radio, television, and digital content platforms.

Propaganda

Propaganda is the production of material designed to further a specific agenda. Techniques include the selective use of information or the presentation of falsehoods as facts.

Propaganda is <u>manipulative</u>.

The truth is: **We need a lesson in brand literacy.**

Media literacy is rightfully at the center of our current debate over how to move toward reestablishing a shared sense of reality.

I would offer _brand literacy_ as another useful discipline that might help us take a look behind the media, at the actors with the actual agendas: the brands themselves.

While it is hard enough to keep afloat in the stormy, chaotic ocean of brands we find ourselves treading in, it can be even harder to decipher the true intention of certain brands.

That intention can be helpful in decoding the media-brand relationship.

~~Nike~~ wants us to buy a lifestyle,
but it sells apparel.

~~HBO~~ wants us to buy TV shows,
but it sells commercials.

~~Chevrolet~~ wants us to buy freedom,
but it sells transportation.

~~Amazon~~ wants us to buy delight,
but it mines data.

~~Netflix~~ wants us to buy content,
but it sells subscriptions.

~~Disney~~ wants us to buy happiness,
but it sells tickets.

~~CNN~~ wants us to buy journalism,
but it sells advertising.

~~Facebook~~ wants us to buy belonging,
but it sells our privacy.

The truth is: **We need citizens, not consumers.**

We have been trained exceptionally well in the art of consumerism.

Sparkly Super Bowl spots find their way into our social media feeds, spinning heartwarming tales of gifting your spouse a car for Christmas.

We are told that our purchasing power is the fuel that makes our economic superiority the envy of all. We're even made to believe that it is _our responsibility_ to spend money because we contribute to the good of all.

And sure, there may be some truth in that.
Giving presents feels good.

"_Education is the foundation of good citizenship._"

– NIKOLE HANNAH-JONES

At the same time, we seem helplessly uneducated in the art of citizenship.

Some brands are only functional if the majority of a population feels like it belongs to them. Democracy is one such brand. And it takes informed and engaged citizens to keep it thriving.

It takes pushing back against those who seek to limit that circle of belonging. And it requires participants who accept their responsibility in good faith contributions—through taxes, through honest discourse and exchange of ideas.

It is only through the contribution of all that a social system functions at all.

The next generation needs to be reeducated on the basic mechanisms that make communal living in a society possible.

The truth is: **We need to —(un)plug the Matrix.**

Social media has turned life into performance art.

And its facilitators make astronomical profits from it. It's like a gallery arranged an exhibition of our lives and takes 100 percent of the sales.

Our lives. On display.

Worse yet, the gallery has set up a public messaging board that lets anyone share their thoughts and opinions, without checking facts or verifying identities. That's not to say we can't use Facebook to connect with our high school friends. Sure, let's do that.

Book of faces? Great.
Web of falsehoods? Anything but that.

And yes, it baffles the mind
this wasn't anticipated.

The truth is: **We need brands* to do better.**

Whether it's a commitment to treating our employees better, cutting our emissions by choice, or building a more sustainable supply chain, there are countless ways for brands to make a positive impact on all of us.

In a world where it seems increasingly harder to trust our leaders to do right by all of us, it falls on brands to fill that vacuum and do better for each of us.

We have surrendered the public square to them, so it's only fair to ask them to maintain it, sweep, pick up the trash, and make sure everyone is still welcome.

We need them to tear up the worst in us. And unite us around the good that's at the core of most of us.

*That means everybody who participates in the public discourse.

LEVI STRAUSS & CO.

TRADE   MARK

In the mid 1950s, Levi's strongarmed the community of Blackstone, Virginia, into racially integrating their factory through the threat of closure. The company rejected the town's proposed "compromises" of building walls, drawing lines across their factory floors, even separate drinking fountains.

In the end, town leadership relented. And the world is better for it.

Yes to better Brands©

We need to build more brands of <u>belonging.</u>

A great brand is like a magnet. It attracts attention from individuals and communities, bringing them together through the proposition of value.

And, in most cases, it delivers on that value along a spectrum of satisfaction to the consumer. And if that satisfaction is high—and the value great—our emotional connection to that brand will be strong.

And that connection is crucial to our lives.

& Branding.

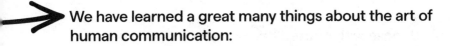

➤ We have learned a great many things about the art of human communication:

* *The articulation and recording of thought*
* *The purposeful shaping of ideas for public circulation*
* *The frictionless distribution to a global audience*

And yes, branding offers us robust tools for large-scale human connection and collaboration.

> *"This is an age of mass production [. . .] In this age, too, there must be a technique for the mass distribution of ideas."*
>
> **– EDWARD BERNAYS**

Branding is not the answer. It is the <u>key.</u>

A key is a simple tool. Whether it's a rusty piece of iron or a laser-cut blade of aluminum, its function remains the same: *It unlocks things.*

Branding by no means will fix what ails us. But good branding will make good ideas and products strong and stealthy. It will give them the chance of attracting attention.

And those well-crafted brands can open doors and get us into the rooms we need to get into. And sure, once inside, we are left to deal with its contents: It might be complex, joyful, messy, toxic, or abandoned.

But without getting inside, the contents of each and every room will elude us. Possibly forever.

Branding is <u>key</u> to the future we imagine.

Whether it's our **<u>5G</u>** wireless networks that will power not just the internet of things but also the internet of ideas, the adoption of a more ***humane capitalism*** with the human at its core, or our acceptance (finally!) of the unfolding ***climate crisis***, branding plays a key role in wrapping our heads around complex issues.

Yet, to do so, we need to find a way to get our heads out of the unrelenting information cycle.

> *"There is nothing as anti-utopian as the product we call the news. Let your interest be expansive. Read philosophy and psychology. Look around and think, It doesn't have to be this way."*
>
> **– RUTGER BERGMAN** / The New York Times

We need to create space from brands, so we can focus on branding.

Less streams from the cloud. More head in the clouds.

325

We need to fill that space with growing awareness. Because it is not enough for a select few to be woke.

We need to awaken the MASSES!

We need to reignite our sense of belonging. Not what belongs to us, but what and who we belong to.

Which, admittedly, is hard. Especially when many of us are stuck inside the Matrix, in a fever dream of disinformation.

But.

IF NOT NOW, THEN WHEN?
IF NOT US, THEN WHO?

Many of these issues cannot wait.
Or it will be too late.

ALL AWAKE NOW ALL AWAKE NOW ALL AWAKE NOW ALL AWAKE NOW

Thankfully, the alarm has gone off.
And we are waking up.

Socially.
Politically.
Economically.
Racially.
Environmentally.
Individually.
Collectively.

GEORGE
FLOYD

*Some, however, are set on
hitting the snooze button.*

SNOOZE

WO:KE

Against every cultural movement, there seems to be the inevitable backlash. Like waves descending on a beach, forward, backward—sometimes violently crashing, sometimes gently gliding across the sand— we go up and down, back and forth, high and low.

Constantly. Naturally. Perpetually.

And yes, the critics of *"woke culture"* are plentiful.

The political and cultural right has hijacked the term and stuffed it with every facet of their grievance— social justice, police reform, science, critical race theory, and, of course, *"cancel culture."*

On the left, criticism is lobbed especially against the movement's perceived absolutist views—a kind of litmus test of progressive purity.

The sentencing of this kind of *"internet justice"* often takes shape as a mob on social media and has led to people losing their jobs, reputations, and livelihoods for minor misdeeds, sometimes decades old.

This certain kind of *"woke capitalism"* is often heavy on virtue signaling but light on virtue fulfillment and looks at the support of social causes and equity and inclusion pledges mainly as a marketing strategy.

"And so the young adherents of the Great Awokening exhibit the zeal of the Great Awakening [. . .] they punish heresy by banishing sinners from society or coercing them to public demonstrations of shame [. . .] We have the cult of social justice on the left, a religion whose followers show the same zeal as any born-again Evangelical."

– ANDREW SULLIVAN

Yet "hate culture" is real.
It comes in Small, Medium, and Large.

As a society—as a species—we have to stop accepting orders for super-sized servings of hate because hate will turn into calamity almost without fail. We simply cannot keep waiting for tragedies to move us to the streets. It is way past time for leaders who offer thoughts and prayers but no action.

Thoughts and prayers may help them find the courage to look into the mirror every morning, but this emotional carousel is useless for the rest of us. They are two hollow words with a conjunction in between.

We need sustained, systemic reasons for hope. We need more brands that are taking stands.

And no. It is not enough to simply say that you're better than everybody else. Anybody can do that.

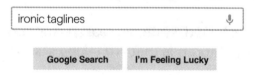

And no, primary brand colors don't make this anything to chuckle at.

We need our actions to match our words AND our symbols.

A mask only works if worn correctly.

A black square is only useful as part of a larger, active conversation about the rights of Black citizens.

A rainbow banner on your LinkedIn page is only as good as your anti-discrimination policies.

A symbol for social distancing is only authentic if a company is committed, at its core, to protecting its workers and customers.

And an altruistic tagline only works if, well, you don't allow your algorithms to disseminate tutorials of terrorism, enable hate speech, or serve up up fact-free political propagandas.

"Watch what they do. Not what they say."

– RACHEL MADDOW

Let's brand the _NEW_ and _NOW_.

We now have the power to build brands around forces for good with the stroke of a pen. With the push of a computer key. The command of our voice.

And we have the ability to reach people in locations and at scales unlike any other time in history.

All that is needed is a purpose that resonates, that has emotional substance. And people will follow.

Online.
In the streets.
At the ballot box.
And, ultimately, in the courtrooms.

BLACK LIVES MATTER

HYPEROBJECTS

Timothy Morton, professor of literature and the environment at the University of California, Davis, coined the term *hyperobjects* to describe entities that are so massively distributed in time and space, they tend to elude a tangible specificity, like race or class, or climate change.

#METOO

And no, not all new brands are equally successful at capturing people's attention.

Let's rebrand the _TRIED_ and _TIRED_.

Every day, in every corner of our little speck of the universe, people are working to redefine themselves, redefine ideas, or redefine one industry or another.

They are working on the next big idea. On the next new brand that will change the way we live, the way we shop, and the way we relate to each other. It might change the way we love.

And they use branding to turn those ideas into reality.

But many of the things that desperately need the tools of branding are things that are old—perceptions, terms, and ideas that have hardened into outdated ways of thinking, doing, and making.

Often, these are definitions that send misleading messages or expressions rooted in histories of oppression.

Ch~~AAA~~eader

~~Socialism.~~

Humanism?

~~Grandfathered In~~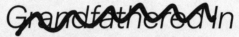

In some Southern states, voters encountered easier voting conditions if they had a grandfather who had voted before 1867. This disenfranchised Black voters, because their ancestors had been slaves and not able to vote.

~~Global Warming.~~

Climate ~~Change?~~

Climate Crisis!

~~Sold Down the River~~

This expression derives from America's history of slavery. Slaves were sold "down river," where they would experience harsher conditions, as punishment.

~~Locker Room Talk.~~

Harassment?

~~Basket Case~~

This is WWI slang and refers to soldiers who were so seriously injured you could fit them in a basket.

~~Housewife~~

It sounds simple. But it's complex. Of course.

Most of these issues are — unlike this book — not black or white. Most everything lives in that dreaded zone of gray, the one that doesn't provide a clear path to the right answer.

Sure, more electric vehicles on the road sounds like a good idea, especially when they're nicely branded with a leaf and, most likely, come in a nice, vibrant shade of green. A color that reminds us of nature hikes and taps into outdoor nostalgia.

Yet, what if the electricity it runs on is generated by burning fossil fuels? How about the energy needed to produce this green fleet? Where does that come from? And how about all the perfectly drivable cars out there? Does it make sense to replace them all?

Damn you, rabbit holes!

It is easy to see how the complexities of life end up leaving us overwhelmed and susceptible to stories of the wild and mighty. It is easy for them to drown out the mundane and taxing decisions that make up most of our lives.

Helpless. Hopeless. Hamsters.

Spinning. Galloping.

It is often said that simplicity tops complexity. That it leads to the most likely solution, the most reasonable explanation.

This is true for life. And for branding.

And the simplest thing I can think of is this:

Let's amplify symbols of <u>hope</u>!

And abolish
symbols
of ha̶t̶e.

See with Love.

Speak with Love.

We were destined to become a reflection of the mediums we shape. And the world we have constructed—despite its possibly fatal flaws and stupendous shortcomings—is still the most radically transparent and egalitarian framework we have yet conceived.

Everything and every person has, theoretically, access to the public square.

Which means that everything that enters that square—which is nearly everything—needs to be articulated, shaped, and framed with purpose.

Yes, everything needs to be branded.

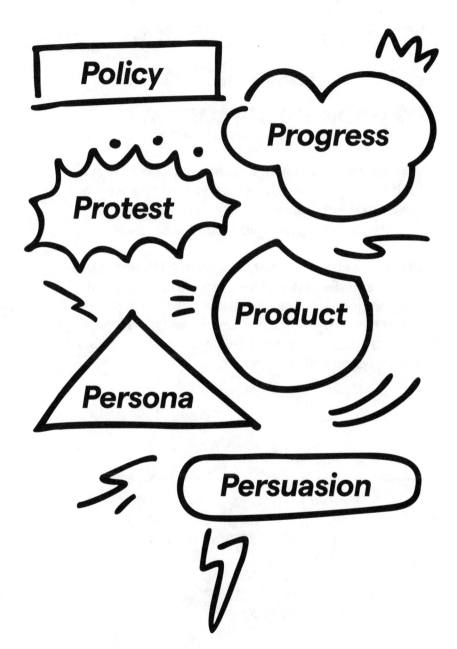

We find ourselves at a crossroads: **This is the age of peak opportunity.**

With existential challenge comes monumental opportunity. We're in the midst of redefining how we work. How we govern ourselves. What kind of planet we leave to the next generation of humans.

We have a chance to determine which labels to use, invent, and discard. And yes, branding will play an even bigger part in our existence than it has so far. And the next generation of brands will have to embrace this change the same way our current societies are grappling with adapting to it.

HATE
HAS NO
BUSINESS
HERE.

NO MORE THOUGHTS & PRAYERS

ALL AWAKE NOW ALL AWAKE NOW ALL AWAKE NOW

HUMAN KIND HUMAN KIND HUMAN KIND

Let's evolve from branding goods to BRANDING <u>GOOD</u>.

The experiences produced by brands, at their most powerful, put us in touch with the mighty, the mythic, and the eternally symbolic. They provide helpful fictions, aspirational images, and simple, emotionally resonant narratives that help us comprehend our reality—or augment it to our liking.

There have always been inseparable connections between the world's peoples—common symbols and common understandings. As ever, we continue to reinterpret and reignite those symbols. We link them to our struggles, make them stand-ins of our hopes.

BRANDING
GOOD
WITH GOOD BRANDING

It is time we use branding for good,
and brands for a purpose, not just profit.

Branding inspires us to dream, to imagine.

We look to brands like stars, lighting our path to being, becoming, and belonging.

AWAKE

Update Now…

Acknowledgments

Thanks to my wife Gretchen, who accepts my obsessions and anxieties.

Thanks to my sons Quinn & Paxton, who give me hope for the future.

Thanks to my partner David, who continues to support my creative detours.

Thanks to my siblings Felix, Eva, and Simon, who give me roots despite physical distance.

Thanks to my parents Regula & Rudolf, who conceived a mostly productive fusion of art and science.

Thanks to my initial collaborator Erica, who helped me build a sturdy structural foundation.

Thanks to my friend Daniel, who figured out what this book is about.

Thanks to my editor Ava, who balances guidance and guardrails with encouragement and empathy.

Thanks to my executive editor Jessica, who let me make changes long after the official process permitted.

Thanks to the team at Greenleaf, who manages a delicate process with competence and kindness.

Thanks to Kesley at Greenleaf, who recognized value in my unsolicited proposal.

Thanks to the family of creative humans, who continue to inspire me to become a better creative human.

Visual Credits

P.9 **"Man Walking in the Night"**: iStock.com/rancescoch • *P.19* Composite of **"Fish Engraving"**: iStock.com/bauhaus1000 • *P.21* **"Man Thinking Underwater Observing Clouds"**: iStock.com/rancescoch • *P.24* **"Antique XIX Century Engraving of a Jersey Bull"**: iStock.com/NSA Digital Archive • *P.27* Composite of **"Coke vs. Pepsi"**: iStock.com/omersukrugoksu and iStock.com/radub85 • P.29 **"Antique Cabinet Card Photograph of Gentlemen in Beaver Top Hats"**: Kingsley Studio, public domain via Wikimedia Commons • *PP.38/39* **"NYC Billboard Ad For Supreme Skate Fashion"**: iStock.com/CribbVisuals • *P.41* **"Barbara Kruger"** by Rich_Lem: licensed under CC BY-NC-SA 2.0 • *PP.44/45* **"Woman Looking at her Face in Shards of Broken Mirror Pieces"**: iStock.com/AOosthuizen • *P.49* **"Person Hands Hold US Passports on a White Background"**: iStock.com/samiylenko • *P.51* **"Young American Students Pledging Allegiance to the Flag"**: iStock.com/JBryson • *P.56* **"Portrait of a Beautiful Young Woman"** by HEX with permission from Tobias Prasse • *P.59* **"Funny Cartoon Cats"**: iStock.com/Svetlana_Smirnova • *P.60* **"A Couple in a Music Group Dancing beside a Train"** by HEX with permission from Tobias Prasse • *P.66* **"Hamburger Eat-ing Lazy Couch Potato"**: iStock.com/sumnersgraphicsinc • *P.67* **"This Is the Life!"**: iStock.com/PeopleImages • *P.69* **"Young Lonely Man Walk in Desert on the Sand Texture"**: iStock.com/Михаил Руденко • / *P.71* **"Naptime Office Worker"**: iStock.com/RyanJLane • *P.74* **"Crowds Cheering on a Sports Stadium"**: iStock.com/vm • *P.75* **Liver Bird** has been a symbol of Liverpool for over 800 years; **You'll Never Walk Alone** Song Title by Gerry and the Pacemakers • *P.76* **"Aerial View of Highway and Overpass in City on a Cloudy Day"**: iStock.com/c1a1p1c1o1m1 • *P.79* **"Hacker Standing Alone in Dark Room"**: iStock.com/FOTOKITA • *PP.80/81* **"Red Pill Blue Pill Concept"**: iStock.com/ Diy13 • *P.82* Composite with **"White Rat Standing on Two Legs"**: iStock.com/Thomas Leirikh • *P.85* Composite with **"Bison | Antique Animal Illustrations"**: iStock. com/NSA Digital Archive • *P.87* **"Two Poor Children, Brother With Toy"**: iStock.com/Ruslanshug • *P.89* Composite with **"Antique Engraving of a Cherub"**: iStock.com/NSA Digital Archive and **NIKE SWOOSH** by Carolyn Davidson • *P.89* Composite with **"Grim Reaper Medieval Drawing Of Death 16th Century"**: iStock. com/Grafissimo and **NIKE SWOOSH** by Carolyn Davidson • *P.92* **"Teen Behind the Cage"**: iStock.com/coffee-kai • *P.93* **"Ecological Catastrophy"**: iStock.com/ Максим Шмаков • *P.97* Excerpt of **The Matrix** by Lilly & Lana Wachowski • *P.105* **"Cave on the Nullarbor Plain, Australia"**: iStock.com/Totajla • *P.106* **"Campfire in the Cave"**: iStock.com/Kamila Kozioł • *P.108* **"Cueva de las Manos, pinturas rupestres antiguas de Patagonia, Argentina en Bajo Caracoles"**: iStock.com/Buenaventuramariano • *P.112* **Apple Emojis** • *P.117* **"Nilgiri South"**: iStock.com/jankovoy • *P.122* **"Pyramid of the Stones"**: iStock.com/Viktor_Gladkov • *P.124* **"The Word 'Stay' on the Sand of the Beach"**: iStock.com/Daniar Rahmasari • *P.129* **"Woman Showing ASL Alphabet on White Background"**: iStock.com/OvsiankaStudio • *P.131* **"A**

Rustic and Shabby Chic Breakfast Room": iStock.com/ nicolamargaret • *P.132* **"Watercolor Drawing Apple"**: iStock.com/car_arch_angel • *P.135* **"Declaration of Independence (1819)"**: by John Trumbull via Wikimedia Commons • *PP.136/137* Composition with **"Two Universal Blank Closed A4, (A5) Brochures with Soft Realistic Shadows Isolated on Gray Background"**: iStock.com/ OlegPhotoR • *P.138* **"Letterpress Yes"**: iStock.com/ RTimages • *P.143* **"Logo of Bass Brewery's Pale Ale from 1876"** via Wikimedia Commons • *P.146* **"Identification Bracelet"**: iStock.com/Ziviani • *P.147* **"Beautiful Young Woman on Grey Background"**: iStock.com/ izusek • *P.148* **"Vintage John F. Kennedy Political Campaign Button"**: iStock.com/NoDerog • *PP.162/163* **"Two Women Whispering a Gossip Secret to Each Other"**: iStock.com/Slphotography • *P.167* **"African Mid Age Man Portrait with Beard"**: iStock.com/SensorSpot • *P.176* **"Nothing Brightens Your Life Like Travel"**: iStock. com/PeopleImages • *P.179* **"Christ Gothic"**: iStock. com/Halamka • *P.180* **"Scared Housewife"**: iStock.com/ SaulHerrera • *P.184* **"Auschwitz II—Birkenau—Death Camp—Processing Center—Family Photo of Jewish Couple with Star of David Armbands—Oswiecim, Poland"** by Adam Jones, PhD—Global Photo Archive is licensed under CC BY-SA 2.0 • *P.185* **"Back View Portrait of a Woman with a Cross Tattoo"**: iStock.com/ Rawpixel • *P.186* **Coca-Cola Logo** by Frank M. Robinson • *P.188* **"I Heart NY"** by Milton Glaser • *P.189* **Maserati Logo** by Mario Maserati & Ubaldo Righi • *P.190* **Dove Logo** by Ian Brignell • *P.195* **McDonald's Logo** by Jim

Schindler ● *P.195* **Amazon "Smile Logo"** by Turner Duckworth ● *P.197* **Facebook "Like Button"** by Facebook ● *P.197* Take on **"Just Do It"** Tagline by Nike, Inc. ● *P.203* **"Alternative Lifestyle Young Friends Portrait"**: iStock.com/FG Trade ● *P.203* **"Woman Dancing"** by HEX with permission from Tobias Prasse ● *P.203* **"Portrait of Cheerful Man with Deer Elk Antlers"**: iStock. com/ Deagreez ● *P.205* **"Young Hipster Couple with Long Curly Hair Kissing at Sunset"**: iStock.com/oleg-breslavtsev ● *P.207* **"Protect Me from What I Want"** by Luca Pedrotti is licensed under CC BY-NC-SA 2.0 ● *P.213* **Celtic Cross** credited to St. Patrick ● *P.213* **"QAnon"** Logo ● *P.213* **"Sunwheel"** Ancient European Symbol ● *P.216* **"Football Fans Clapping on the Podium of the Stadium"**: iStock.com/ALFSnaiper ● *P.218* **"Masonic Pyramid Construction"**: iStock.com/xochicalcoe ● *PP.220/221* **"Man Wearing Blue Jeans Shirt and Showing Blank White Business Card"**: iStock.com/ Pinkypills ● *P.220* **Department of Homeland Security Seal**, developed with input from senior DHS leadership, employees, and the US Commission on Fine Arts and the consulting company Landor Associates ● *P.222* **Logo for Swiss Agency for Development and Cooperation SDC** ● *P.222* **Department of Homeland Security Seal**, developed with input from senior DHS leadership, employees, and the US Commission on Fine Arts and the consulting company Landor Associates ● *P.222* **Reduced Emblem of the KGB**; this work is not an object of copyright according to article 1259 of Book IV of the Civil Code of the Russian Federation No. 230-FZ of December 18, 2006 • *P.226* **HOPE wordmark** based on the "O" logo by Sender LLC design firm: Sol Sender, Amanda Gentry, and Andy Keene • *P.227 Adapted* **"MAGA Cap Design"** • *P.228* **Star & Crescent**, occasionally embraced by Arab nationalism or Islamism • *P.228* **Cross**, symbol of Christianity recalling the crucifixion of Jesus Christ • *P.235* Composition with **"Milky Way"**: iStock.com/Apiruk • *P.239* **"Mysterious Man"**: iStock.com/Alpgiray Kelem • *P.241* **"Katrina Destruction"**: iStock.com/jhgrigg • *P. 249* **"Female Cyborg Looking at Camera"**: iStock.com/max-kegfire • *P.253* **"Martin Winterkorn 2014-03-13"** by Volkswagen AG is licensed under CC BY 3.0 • *P.253* **Volkswagen Logo**, official origin unknown, possibly designed by Franz Xaver Reimspeiss and/or Nikolai Borg • *P.253* **ABC Logo** by Paul Rand • *P.254* **"Louis CK 2012 Shankbone 3"** by david_shankbone is licensed under CC BY 2.0 • *P.254 New York Times* **Logo** *by Edward Benguit* • *P.265* Composition with **"Antique Gold Frame"**: iStock.com/Rouzes • *P.275* Composition of **"Duel of Toy Soldiers"**: iStock.com/messenjah and **"Medieval Man at Arms"**: iStock.com/duncan1890 • *P.277* **"Human therefore Kind"**: composition based on **"Man Wearing Blue Jeans Shirt and Showing Blank White Business Card"**: iStock.com/Pinkypills • *P.279* **"Chicken Farm"**: iStock.com/pidjoe • *P.279* **"This One's All Mine"**: iStock.com/pixdeluxe • *P. 280* **"Big Hand and Cartoon Man"**: iStock.com/NLshop • *P.281* **"Gargoyle Shadow"**: iStock.com/draco77 and **"Cartoon Sad Tree Trunk and Lumberjack Cutting a Forest"**: iStock.com/NLshop • *P.283* **"Am I Next? Stu-**

dent Lie-In at the White House to Protest Gun Laws" by Lorie Shaull is licensed under CC BY-SA 2.0 • *P.285* **"The Rising Sun in the Arctic"**: iStock.com/sodar99 • *P.289* Composition with **"Two Universal Blank Closed A4, (A5) Brochures with Soft Realistic Shadows Isolated on Gray Background"**: iStock.com/OlegPhotoR and **"Evil Skull-Octopus Mascot"**: iStock.com/Serhii Yakovliev • *P.297* Composite of **"Nilgiri South"**: iStock.com/jakovoy *and* **"Environmental Protection Worker in an Orange Hazmat Suit"**: iStock.com/bokan76 • *P.299* **"Milky Way"**: iStock.com/Apiruk • *P.303* **Twitter Logo** by Twitter designer Douglas Bowman • *P.303* **Facebook Logo** by Mike Buzzard of Cuban Council • *P.303* **Google Logo** by Google designers, original logotype by Ruth Kedar • *P.317* Composition with **"Levi's Strauss Logo - Jim Crow Cover"**• *PP.326/327* **"Rage Against the Machine"** by Fabrice Trombert • *P.328* Composite of **"Man Hand with Various Gestures"**: iStock.com/Vlajko611 *and* **"Clock Alarm Radio Hope"**: iStock.com/Olivier Verriest • *P.330* **"Three Coffee Cups Sized Small, Medium, and Large"**: iStock.com/gbrundin *P.335* **"Black Lives Matter, traced"** spotted on Myrtle Ave., BK • *P.335* **"Defund the Police, traced"** spotted on Myrtle Ave., BK

all awake now
all awake now
all awake now
all awake now
all awake now
all awake now
all awake now
all awake now
all awake now
all awake now
all awake now
all awake now
all awake now
all awake now
all awake now
all awake now
all awake now
all awake now